Leading with Empathy and Grace

Secrets to Developing High-Performing Teams

Tammy Harkins Klotz

© 2024 Tammy Harkins Klotz

All Rights Reserved. Except for brief quotations included in critical reviews and certain other noncommercial uses allowed by copyright law, no part of this publication may be reproduced, distributed, or transmitted in any form or by any means, including photocopying, recording, or other electronic or mechanical methods, without the publisher's prior written permission. Write to the publisher at the address below, addressing your letter to the "Attention: Permissions Coordinator," requesting permission.

Disclaimer

While the publisher and author have taken every precaution to ensure that the information in this book was accurate at the time of publishing, they do not accept responsibility for any errors, inaccuracies, omissions, or other inconsistencies that may be present. They also disclaim any liability to any party for any loss, damage, or disruption that may be caused by any errors or omissions, regardless of whether they are the result of negligence, accident, or other causes.

All names, characters, companies, locations, events, and incidents in this book, unless otherwise noted, are either imaginary or the result of the author's imagination. Any likeness to real people, living or dead, or to real things is entirely coincidental.

Reviews and Praise

"This is simply a must-read leadership book. You can spend 20+ years in leadership and not learn half the lessons presented here. Tammy brings these lessons to life with heartfelt storytelling. Every chapter has a wealth of critical messages pertaining to you, the team, the org, development, the lifecycle. I particularly liked the weaved messages on leaders needing team- and self-awareness and care... otherwise you can't be at your best, and expect others to be at their best. These aren't just leadership lessons, but life lessons! If you are a leader, or want to be a leader, you need to read this book."

- **Barry** - – executive leader, coach, advisor, board member

"This is a really great book for aspiring leaders as well as seasoned veterans in any business. Starting with the characteristics of a great leader and high performing teams, to building and developing the team, through evaluating and sustaining performance, this book will guide you through each stage. Tammy is a respected leader with years of experience and she has navigated all the challenges thrown at her - by reading this you will learn the secrets of her success."

- **Bill**

"Leading with Empathy and Grace" is a heartfelt narrative that transcends the traditional leadership manual. Tammy Klotz weaves her journey with universal leadership truths, offering a soul-stirring guide that speaks directly to the heart of every reader. It's not just about leading; it's about touching lives, shaping destinies, and leaving a legacy of kindness, understanding, and unwavering support. This book is a beacon for those aspiring to lead with not just their minds, but with their hearts fully engaged."

- **Kelly**

"Tammy delivers a targeted, relevant, digestible and easy to follow guide for success. She breaks down concepts to actionable and bite-size steps for success".

- **Tonya**

I wanted to take a moment to recommend a fantastic book. It was incredibly well-organized and comprehensive, with clear, concise writing throughout. I especially appreciated the way Tammy used personal anecdotes and feedback from her colleagues to illustrate the key concepts and processes in such an accessible way.

What really stood out to me were the subtleties that were highlighted, which made me appreciate how much attention to detail is required to be a successful leader. I had several "ah hah" moments while reading, and I'm sure others will feel the same way.

The chapter breakdowns were easy to follow and really helped me to drill down on the finer points. I found myself using the table of contents to outline each chapter and create a flowchart of steps and questions to ask to help me build my own high-performing team.

Overall, it was an easy and enjoyable read, and one that I feel has invaluable lessons for anyone in a leadership position. I'll be gifting a copy to my nephew so that he can benefit from Tammy's insights and do some self-reflection on his own work. Additionally, I will be recommending this book to other managers/leaders I know and respect so they might take advantage of the great insights offered in this book.

Thank you, Tammy, for sharing your knowledge and

experiences in such a clear and relatable way. I'm sure your book will continue to help people in their careers for years to come.

- Mark Perlman

I've had the privilege of collaborating with Tammy over the past few years within a professional capacity. From our initial encounter in front of a sizable audience of engineers, technicians, and managers, where she presented a new security initiative, it was evident to me that Tammy possesses exceptional qualities. With over 35 years of experience in engineering and cyber security, I've rarely encountered a leader in Tammy's position who engages with such clarity and openness. Unlike the typical authoritative approach often seen in similar situations, Tammy demonstrated a genuine willingness to listen to concerns and feedback, fostering an environment where communication thrived. Throughout the project, Tammy displayed fearlessness in delving into intricate details and swiftly resolving complex issues. Her leadership style involves surrounding herself with expertise and empowering her team to make decisions, making her a truly unique figure in our industry.

- **Bob Bevis** - COO-Verve Industrial, a Rockwell Company

This book gives you the bang for your buck! It is filled with useful examples and stories to guide your leadership journey. From the types of rewards you can give your employees to how to use decompression sessions, Tammy gives you an instruction manual on how you can lead with empathy. Her personal stories will help to illuminate your path to empathic leadership. Ending each chapter with a "message to you", Tammy acknowledges that this is not easy work but THIS is the work that is required to lead. Tammy ends her book by reminding us that great leaders, great teams, and great organizations thrive with a human touch. If you are ready to engage yours, this book is for you!--Jill Helmer, Executive, Team and Organization Development Coach

Great job! You really poured your heart and soul into this book and I know it will help many to find their path. Thank you for being so brave. I am proud of you!

- Jill Helmer

Dedication

To my daughters: Samantha Jo and Erin Beth

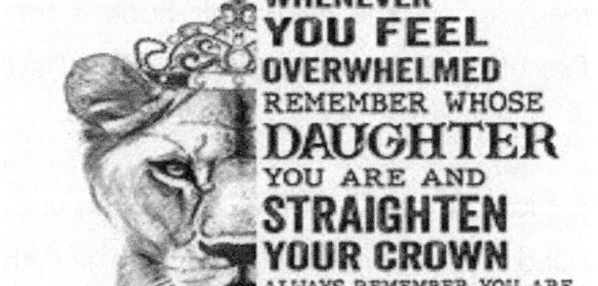

- Unknown Source: Zazzle[1]

---

[1] Zazzle. "My Daughter Canvas Print | Zazzle". (n.d.). https://www.pinterest.com/pin/358880664064856891

Contents

Foreword	1
Preface	4
Acknowledgments	13
Introduction	15
Chapter 1 - Building a High-Performing Team	19
The Leader	20
The Differences between a Leader and a Manager	21
The 25 Qualities of Great Leaders	23
Your Personal Life	50
Building Effective Leadership Qualities	52
The Team	55
Qualities of a Great Team	56
Understanding Your Team	57
Diversity, Equity / Equality, and Inclusion	57
The Organization	62
Organizational Culture	63
Business / Market Forces	65
My Message to You	69
Chapter 2 - Getting The Right People on Your Bus	71
Choosing Where to Serve (The Leader)	72

Why Join a Team	72
Taking Up a Challenge	73
Creating Your Team	76
Understand the Purpose and Mission	77
Criteria for Hiring	77
Preparing for the Interview	80
The Documentation	81
The Interview	82
Selecting a Candidate	84
Making the Offer	86
Optimizing pre-existing teams	89
Roles and Responsibilities	90
Understand The Team	92
Identify the Gaps	94
Onboarding	97
The Welcome	97
Orientation	99
Embed in the Team	100
Offboarding	101
Transition Plan	102
Timing	105
The Exit	106
My Message to You	110
Chapter 3 - Developing Your Team	**113**
Operating Principles	114
Principle #1:Transparency	114

Principle #2: Togetherness	115
Principle #3: Inclusion	115
Principle #4: Presence	115
Principle #5: Participation	116
Principle #6: Consistency	116
Stages of Team Development	117
Forming	119
Storming	120
Norming	122
Performing	123
Continuous Improvement (Adjourning)	125
Interaction Levels	127
Group Level	128
One to One	134
Accountability Partners	141
Decompression Sessions	147
Managing Up	150
My Message to You	153
Chapter 4 - Collaborating with Partners	**155**
Partnering with Internal and External Stakeholders	156
Internal Stakeholders	156
External Stakeholders	158
Defining Roles	167
RACI Chart	167
Shared Accountability Matrix	170
The Service Contract	170

Making Stakeholders "Part of the Team"	171
Maintaining Stakeholder Relationships	173
Weekly and Monthly Meetings	174
Quarterly Business Reviews	176
Managing Perception	176
Measuring Performance	178
Trending	180
Validation	181
My Message to You	185
Chapter 5 - Sustaining a High Performing Team	**187**
Characteristics of High-Performing Teams	188
Grace	189
Safety	195
Reciprocity	196
Resilience	197
Maintaining Alignment of the Team's Goals and Objectives	199
Setting Team Goals and Objectives	199
Getting S.M.A.R.T.	201
Understanding Team Members' Career Aspirations	205
Providing Development and Performance Feedback	209
Specificity over Generalization	211
Make it Bi-directional	211
Motivating Team Members	213
Applying the Golden Rule	213
Money Isn't Everything	214
Share the Positivity	214

Making Motivational Moments	215
Avoiding Demotivational Moments	220
Managing Transformational Change	221
Alignment Versus Agreement	221
Stakeholder Analysis	225
Planning for Continuity	226
Driving a Healthy Narrative	227
Dealing with Stress	228
Self-care	230
Decompression Sessions	231
My Message to You	232
Chapter 6 - Performance	**235**
Excellent Performance	237
Response	237
Recognition	238
Rewards	243
Good Performance	246
Response	247
Poor Performance	249
Response	250
Remediation	253
Consequences	254
Documentation	260
Improvement Opportunities	260
My Message to You	262
Chapter 7 - Self-Care	**265**

Knowing Your Boundaries	268
Work-Life Balance	271
Physical Care	279
Mental & Emotional Care	280
Small Stuff	281
Big Stuff	283
Work Stuff	286
My Message to You	287
Conclusion	**289**
Glossary	**294**
About the Author	**296**

Foreword

I have known Tammy Klotz for several years now and I have found her to not only be a skilled technologist, which is her expertise, but a leader of leaders. I say this confidently because as much skill as she has in her subject matter expertise, her ability to lead others and make them better is second to none. I have watched this firsthand, this is her superpower, which I will call "Tammy's Teachings". I have watched her reach awesome success in her career, start and lead a senior leader cyber-security group that collaborates and shares best practices, and write this book on leadership. From the moment I picked up the book to read I was captivated, enlightened, and encouraged to do better and will leverage the teachings as a go to guide of everyday leadership and life.

This seven-chapter book begins with leadership qualities chronicled and where servant

Leadership is personified with many tips describing not only how to implement these qualities but outlining how to live them to be extraordinary leaders and people. This beginning sets the tone for us as we step through the chapters where we can imagine ourselves in an utopian business setting.

The middle chapters are truly a blueprint to not only reshaping yourself, but your team's ability to increase productivity, enhance efficiency, and enjoy each other in a high energy positive culture that many of us yearn for. This is imperative from a perspective of building teams, hiring for the right culture fit, performance enhancement, and building partnerships, while building a collaborative approach where everybody wins.

Tammy sets the level of transforming teams in an easy-to-read step by step framework that will work in every organizational setting and life situation.

This book in my mind should be read over a seven-week journey and with each chapter read weekly while absorbing the content and lived during that week.

This incredible leadership and life guide should be enjoyed every quarter to reinforce our life's work using "Tammy's Teachings," but more importantly make us better human beings that make a difference in our lives and every person with whom we interact.

Written By:

Angelo J. Valletta,

President and CEO

Ben Franklin Technology Partners of Northeastern PA

Preface

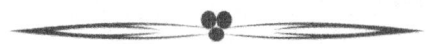

I remember the interaction, the location, and the ask vividly... "Tammy, teach people how to lead as you do". Quizzically, I looked at my boss, who posed the challenge and said, "It's who I am. I'm not sure I know how to teach someone to be like me." It was early in my leadership journey, but he saw something in me that he wanted others to see and learn. That interaction is the initial inspiration for this book. This book is my 'pay-it-forward' to share my experiences and approach with others to become great leaders!

I started my career straight out of college in 1992. My degree was in Math, Computer Science, and Secondary Education. I wanted to be a math teacher, but the supply of teachers far exceeded the demand at that time. So I changed course, and I started my career in corporate America. I worked for a large industrial gas and chemical manufacturing company that afforded me many different opportunities, given the size of the company and the career development program they offered. I spent my first few years in individual contributor roles, learning the business and figuring out how this 'job thing' worked. In 1997, I started on my leadership journey, managing a small team of four individuals responsible for computer hardware and software deployments for ~3000 employees. Did I have what it took to be a leader in Corporate America? Heck, I was going to be a math teacher! As you can imagine, I had a lot to learn and a lot to prove. Perhaps mostly, I had a lot to prove to myself. Was I up to the challenge? Could I really lead teams effectively in a fast-paced environment that was alien to what I was used to? Though I didn't step into this role naively, the leadership experience that followed certainly presented to me more than I could ever have imagined. Thankfully, throughout my twenty-one years in the IT organization, I was blessed with many role models (some positive, some not so positive). I held 8 different leadership positions over those 21 years, worked with many different types of individuals, and worked for many different types of bosses: some leaders and some managers. I had a cast of supporters within the organization who believed in me and my leadership abilities. I recognized the opportunity and accepted the challenge. I learned many lessons, built and transformed teams, and ultimately established myself as a successful and respected leader in the IT organization.

During those same 21 years, my personal life presented many situations that contributed to the challenges of being a successful leader. I lost my dad. I became the primary caregiver for my surviving parent with a cancer diagnosis. I got married and helped raise two stepdaughters in a less-than-pleasant co-parenting environment. I had my first daughter, followed by a miscarriage, which was trumped by my husband being diagnosed with terminal brain cancer. Then, I had my 2nd daughter after being told we could not have any more children. I filed for divorce from a terminally ill spouse. I raised two daughters on my own and survived the suicide of the man I thought I was going to marry next. Four years later, I met my third love, who asked me to marry him in 2019 only to have been betrayed by him while writing this book.

Those are just a "few things" that I had to manage while advancing my career. These experiences made me stronger and more determined to be successful. As my therapist then taught me, the only thing in these situations that I could truly control was my actions and reactions to the situations I found myself in. I truly believe that these life experiences helped me grow as a leader who exemplifies fortitude and resilience and leads her teams with empathy.

Because "life happens". We are all imperfect human beings who deserve some grace in our journeys to become the best we can at the things we are the most passionate about.

After those 'development and formative years', I decided to pivot out of my comfort zone. My boss approached me about an opportunity outside of IT in the Internal Audit organization. My response was, "Really?". My supporting cast knew I didn't know much about internal auditing but they still wanted me in this role as the IT Audit Manager. From my pause, my boss knew I was apprehensive but still saw in me the fullness of what I still was yet to see. Having made great strides and flourished in IT for over two decades, could I truly have the same success in a completely different field? After all, I had a great team. Would I be able to recreate or influence similar dynamics again? As it turned out, my boss had infectious faith in me. I took up the opportunity and never looked back. Making that pivotal change was probably one of my best decisions. I learned so much about business operations in that role, skills I would have never learned in IT. Internal Audit was a different type of organization, less progressive than the IT organization. I was a bit of an 'odd duck' joining the team, so it took a little getting used – bidirectionally, that is, me with them and them with me. The team had its challenges, but with time, it excelled, and the relationships between

Internal Audit and IT teams improved dramatically. The transformation of Audit's being a business partner rather than an adversary was tremendous, and a new level of respect was earned between the organizations. My relationships within the IT organization were foundational to this transformation. Hiring me into that role could have been perceived as a huge risk – after 21 years in IT, I know where all the bodies were buried and where to look to find deficiencies in IT processes and controls. Despite that risk, my leadership wanted me in that role. That, in itself, speaks to the credibility and trust that I had built within the IT team.

Twenty-one years in IT and three in Internal Audit boosted my confidence to continue to grow and move forward. Enter career pivot number two. The company was spinning off one of its business units, and a new IT leadership team was being formed. It was an exciting opportunity, and I wanted to be a part of it. It was risky with many unknowns, but now was the time to test the waters. I talked with the incumbent CIO and decided to interview for one of the positions on the IT Leadership team of the new company. So I did. Only to be told by the CIO that he wanted me on the team but not in the role I interviewed for. He wanted me to lead the cyber security program for the new company. He wanted me to be the Chief Information Security Officer (CISO)!?!? Again, I said... "Really?" He looked at me and said, "You know the business, you have the relationships with the business leaders, you have audit experience, you can learn the rest". And this became the launchpad into my cybersecurity career. While the new company was still being formed, I took the time to learn what I needed to succeed in the CISO role. I studied and earned my CISM, CISSP, and CRISC certifications and successfully performed the role of CISO at not only one but two companies. I built my cybersecurity network in the Philadelphia, PA area, and over my current 7 tenured years as a CISO, I am recognized as an expert in the field and have received many accolades and awards for my contributions to the profession. At the time of writing this book, I started my 3rd CISO role.

Looking back over my now 30+ years of experience (yikes, I can't be that old), I realize that somewhere along the line, as I served as a leader, key leadership concepts 'just clicked' for/in me. Sure, I took leadership classes, but my real-world experience shaped me as I put what I learned into practice. These experiences matched my innate 'human' traits and intuitive nature. It molded me into the leader I am today. My confidence is backed by a proven track record of developing high-performing and functioning teams, the support of my leadership and peer colleagues, the love and patience of my family and friends, and being grounded in my faith. I mention this in this book for professionals because although I trained and studied to be an expert in the roles I have held, I am well-rounded and grounded in my leadership style because of all of the individuals who have helped me become a better human being along the way – my family, my friends, my teammates and team members, my colleagues.

The leaders I hold in high esteem and I share one fundamental belief: to be an effective and impactful leader, you have to be a decent human being or at least have a genuine desire to be one.

So, that's who this book is for: leaders who realize that the workplace isn't filled with robots. It's filled with people worthy of accountability, responsibility, respect, compassion, empathy and grace. Leaders who recognize that the people they work with are someone's daughter, son, mom, dad, husband, wife, brother, sister, partner, and friend. If you realize that it is not enough to treat someone as yet another cog in the wheels of the corporate machine, this book is for you. If you find yourself working at a company that requires you to check your humanity at the door when you arrive and pick it back up when you leave, then keep reading to bring humanity back to the office.

I wrote this book because I found that a human-centered approach to leadership has been far more impactful and fulfilling than any other approach. This book has come into existence now because I know these skills I've acquired and accumulated over the years aren't unique to me. Through all the training and experiences, I offer you everything I've learned. In this book, you will learn how to build teams, lead transformational change, and ensure the sustainability of your teams.

Collaboration is one of the qualities of a great leader you'll read more about that in Chapter One. You should not be surprised that this book was a collaborative effort. Though this book is based on my research, life, and professional experiences, dozens of people in my network (former bosses, friends, industry contacts, past colleagues, and former reporters) were generous enough to work with me and my publisher's writing support team by sharing their invaluable insights. They helped me and my publishers gather many of the insights in this book's pages. They taught me new things that I didn't realize helped them along their journeys. I was overwhelmed with how much value they offered, and I genuinely thank them for making this book a testament to what I believe about the power and performance of great teams and leaders!

I hope everyone who has asked me to teach, coach,

and mentor others on how to be a great leader and build great teams and was left unsatisfied with my previous confused response on how I could achieve this now finds this book a refreshing and satisfying answer to their request.

Acknowledgments

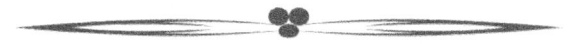

To my managers and leaders: Thank you for providing me with countless lessons and experiences that have shaped me into the leader I am today.

To my colleagues & peers: Thank you for your support and camaraderie through the years.

To my teammates and team members: Thank you for allowing me to mentor and lead you and being part of my high-performing teams.

To my coaches: Thank you for your guidance and patience.

To my book contributors: Thank you for sharing your stories with my Angel Writer to help her 'get me' and learn about our journey together.

To my therapists: Thank you for talking things through with me when I wasn't sure what lesson life was trying to teach me.

To those I have loved hard and lost: Thank you for the seasons we did share and the doors you opened to have conversations about difficult life situations like illness, suicide, and betrayal.

To my closest friends: Thank you for always being there for me, knowing the best and worst about me, and loving me anyway. I would not have survived without each of you picking me up and carrying me along the way when life threw me some unexpected curve balls.

To my parents: Thank you for raising me to be the human being I am today.

To my daughters: Thank you for allowing me to be your mom, teaching you right from wrong, showing you that you can be independent and successful on your own, and loving me unconditionally.

To my Angel Writer and my team at Authors on Mission: Thank you for making my dream of writing my first book come true!!!

To my Book Cover Designer ... thank you for 'getting me' and teaching me to take life 'one bite at a time'.

Introduction

Feeling stuck, stressed, and boxed in is no fun. You dread picking up your phone. The moment you do, you stumble across a crisis that could be handled if the persons responsible only stepped up. No amount of addressing your clear concerns changes anything. You feel the stress the moment you step into the office building. It envelopes you like a cloak that you can't take off. Throughout the day, you resent making follow-ups when your team members know exactly what you need them to do but somehow just don't. Your team performs well sometimes but nowhere near what you believe they can achieve. And you know they are capable of consistently exceptional performance. But what is going on? You rack your brains trying to figure out how to inspire that greatness.

Could it be me? Is there room to be a better leader? Some books and training help, but something is missing.

Something you just can't put your finger on. And if this wasn't enough, you sense your bosses see you struggling to hold things together. They, too, have faith in you and your team. But you are afraid that their faith is waning. You can feel it. This stress and frustration is bearing down on you so much. You feel it affecting your personal life as well. Your family and friends know you're stressed, too. They hear the frustration you share with them. They see it written all over your face, in your voice, and the tension that fills the room when you appear. This isn't the leadership experience you dreamed of or started with! And this is certainly not the leadership experience you want going forward. Everything will fall apart if you don't figure out how to turn things around. You know this.

The good news is that this does not have to be your experience. You can tap into the best of yourself and the best of your team. You can experience consistent high performance from your collective efforts. And you can rise among the ranks in the workforce. You see, this book is the organic product of dozens of former colleagues and stakeholders essentially asking me, "How I do what I do". This book is my "secret sauce," as one colleague labeled it.

With over 30 years of experience in transformational leadership and organization development particularly as an executive in the tech sphere and a thought leader, I offer you lessons I learned directly and from others along the way. The lessons I distilled in this book helped me support teams towards success and rise among the ranks. In this book, I share with you all the lessons I learned and techniques I used that helped me maintain a level of excellence that my teams and I have, over the years, remained proud of. My approach encourages you to embrace your soft skills, particularly the superpower of "empathy," and sometimes fun in realizing organizational goals and team harmony.

Now, I'll be honest with you: some of these things are not easy. Learning and unlearning can be challenging. We both know that. However, everything I'll share with you works. It worked for me, my teams, and some leaders I've had the joy of mentoring over the years. I have complete confidence this book can transform your team. Not only have I seen the results for decades, but I've lived the results, too. I know the joy of going to work daily with calmness and a smile across my face, even in a branch of technology - cybersecurity - that can make many of us anxious at the mere thought of the many challenges we encounter day to day. I also know the joy of picking up my phone and feeling excited to support my team instead of stressed or overburdened. With these approaches I share, you, too, can learn how to create teams where everyone feels a sense of appreciation, ownership, and dedication towards a collective end.

On top of all the above, I imagine you and your loved ones will benefit from the calmness you will enjoy.

So, I invite you to approach this book with an open mind and a practical stance. You will get the most out of this book if you read and diligently apply as you go along.

Are you ready to transform your leadership experience?

Well, it begins with empathy.

Chapter 1

Building a High-Performing Team

Leader + Team + Organization = Greatness

"It's not about me. It never was." - Ted Lasso[2]

Do you enjoy challenges? Well, I certainly do. Especially when it comes to building high-performing teams. It's gratifying for everyone involved. It is, however, also complex and demanding. This chapter explores the elements that make and influence great teams. To help us understand all the aspects we'll look at, I've grouped these elements into three categories: the leader, the team, and the organization. Let's look at the first category: The Leader.

---

[2] Sepinwall, Alan. "'Ted Lasso' Season 3 Finale: The End of a Frustratingly Bad Season" - Season 3 Finale. Rolling Stone. 2023, May 31.
https://www.rollingstone.com/tv-movies/tv-movie-recaps/ted-lasso-season-3-finale-recap-bad-season-jason-sudeikis-brett-goldstein-1234744458/

The Leader

When you think of a great leader, who do you think of? Why do you think of them as that? I assume you are reading this book because you want to be a leader. Perhaps you already are a leader, and you feel there is room to do and be better. If I asked you why "leadership", what would you say? We all have different reasons for choosing leadership or, in some cases, being chosen for it. Some people find that what they enjoy most about leadership are the perks. And, of course, the perks vary. For some, this means health care for themselves and their dependents, annual bonuses, paid leave, a stipend for their kids' school fees, a nice salary, and maybe even a company car. Let's not forget the respect and prestige that a leadership role attracts. Of course, not all leaders get the tangible perks, but all leaders get to enjoy something about leadership. If you ask me what I enjoy most about leadership, it is none of the above.

You see, once you are granted these privileges and start to operate under your leadership role, it may become quite clear to you that there is so much more to being a leader than the perks. For me, the things that make leadership worthwhile are all intangible. I can not begin to quantify the value I receive back, knowing that I've helped people succeed and be successful at what they do. There is something almost "magical" about seeing something click for someone because of your gentle guidance. The closest thing I can compare it to is a "proud mama" moment, and that... that's priceless.

That said, let's agree on what we mean by "leader".

The Differences between a Leader and a Manager

We probably agree with the Dictionary's definition of "leader". A leader is "a person who has commanding authority or influence[3]". When we consider the word "manager", we may even consider these terms almost synonymous. However, a "manager", in my opinion, is often task-oriented, operating in a more compartmentalized and decentralized manner. If a team member performs below agreed expectations, a manager may find it easy to assign blame whilst removing themselves as part of that equation. On the other hand, a "leader" does the opposite. A great leader understands and accepts accountability for their team's overall performance. If one of their direct reports fails to accomplish an agreed goal, the buck doesn't stop at that team member. The buck stops squarely at the feet of that leader. A leader has a strategic perspective and a holistic understanding of their importance as a cog in one of the

---

[3] Merriam-Webster Dictionary. "Leader". 2023, 5th September 2023. https://www.merriam-webster.com/dictionary/leader

wheels that drive the organization forward.

My theory is rooted in the fact that when you have a great team, you don't manage it; you lead it. With a great team, everyone plays their unique role in ensuring the team's and, ultimately, the organization's success. Team members are proactive, responsible, competent, and collaborative. A leader and their team agree on what it takes to do their job. Then that leader gets out of the team's way so they can do that job! And if those team members need assistance at any point, a great leader will roll up their sleeves and give that help. However, team members are competent and supported well enough that these assists are more the exception than the rule. At its best, the overall process is seamless and chugs along as expected.

I particularly found Michael Page's differentiation of "manager" and "leader" helpful[4]. They state that a "Manager" is focused on the administration side of business, whilst a leader's attention is on innovation. When managers are focused on objectives and delegating tasks from a transactional perspective, leaders are eyeing transformational change. They have a vision and are

---

[4] Micheal Page. "Managers vs Leaders: What is the Difference?". https://www.michaelpage.com/advice/management-advice/development-and-retention/managers-vs-leaders-what-difference.

forward-focused. Good managers excel at allocating work and getting things done. But great leaders excel at paying attention to their teams - from a human perspective and empowering them to succeed at the goals set. Managers are power-focused whilst great leaders are influence-focused. When a manager wants to get things done right, expect it to stand firmly in the status quo. When a leader wants to get things done right, expect them to push the boundaries and reshape exactly what that means in light of their convictions that lead them to make changes for the higher good of the team and organization.

The 25 Qualities of Great Leaders

As I explained the difference between the terms "leader" and "manager", I also touched upon some of the important qualities of a great leader. Let me talk to you about the qualities I believe make a great leader. These qualities include self-awareness, empathy, grace, vulnerability, authenticity, approachability, credibility, generosity, creativity, loyalty, and being a good communicator, especially regarding active listening. Let's take a quick look at each of these qualities.

Quality #1: Self-awareness

Most of us are familiar with the concept. And most of us believe that we are self-aware. However, studies tell us that only about 15% of us are self-aware[5]. Did you know that? I was shocked when I found that out. So, With as much self-compassion as is reasonable, take an honest and objective look at yourself. This is important because if your view of yourself is skewed, what's the likelihood that you can fairly assess your team? What's more, your efforts are only part of the equation.

To be an effective leader means being brave and acknowledging where you are in your leadership journey, what work you must do to fit into a new role, and the work you need to do to progress in your existing role or navigate any situation that comes before you. This self-reflection may require you to accept that you may need to upgrade your skills in some ways to become a more effective leader. Your efforts at honestly looking at yourself may direct you to request support from your bosses for additional coaching. In some cases, it may even lead you to request a pause during seasons of your life where you need your career to take a backseat as you navigate pressing challenges in other areas of your life, such as health scares, family emergencies, burn-out, and other curve balls life may throw at you.

---

[5] Eurich, Tasha. "What Self-Awareness Really Is (and How to Cultivate It)". 2018, 4th January. Harvard Business Review. https://hbr.org/2018/01/what-self-awareness-really-is-and-how-to-cultivate-it

According to Harvard Business Review, a balanced level of self-awareness involves a firm grasp of how others see you and how you see yourself[6]. You may wish to take a moment and quietly assess yourself in both regards. Or, you could take a reputable quiz online to help you arrive at an accurate conclusion.

Quality #2: Empathy

"Empathy", is the ability to be aware of the feelings, thoughts, and experiences of others[7] is another crucial trait of effective leaders. Being able to take a moment and reflect on how a situation, action or communication may impact the other person can not only open you up to a whole new layer of understanding but can also help you have smoother relationships with anyone in your work-life and beyond.

I bet you've heard the cliche that kindness costs nothing. We know it's true. However, sometimes it is easy to forget when deadlines are looming, your boss is bearing down on your neck, vendors are failing to perform, and even your home life seems to be a mess. You may feel like you

---

[6] Eurich, Tasha. "What Self-Awareness Really Is (and How to Cultivate It)". 2018, 4th January. Harvard Business Review. https://hbr.org/2018/01/what-self-awareness-really-is-and-how-to-cultivate-it

[7] Merriam Webster. "Empathy". (n.d.). https://www.merriam-webster.com/dictionary/empathy

need kindness just as much as the next guy. But here's the thing, as a leader, your influence can sometimes bear such overarching influence that kindness and support impact someone towards unparalleled performance.

Another aspect that I believe is important when it comes to empathy is that of neutrality. This is especially important in high-tension interactions. When there is conflict, an impartial leader acknowledges and validates everyone's perspectives and views, even if they disagree.

Empathy also breeds and nurtures the presence of inclusivity in a team. Inclusivity is an aspect that all great teams benefit from. When all parties are kept in the loop, and their contribution is acknowledged, invited, and visibly desired, people know they matter. And when people know they matter, they often show up as their best selves in any space. Sometimes, being inclusive shows itself when leaders readily advocate for their team for opportunities with their bosses above them in their organization's hierarchy.

You may consider yourself someone who struggles with displaying or expressing compassion. We are all different. I'm aware that some people aren't predisposed to warm handshakes and broad smiles. And you know what? That's okay. But I am tempted to say that you can at least be fair. Honestly ask yourself, "If this was happening to me, would I find it fair?".

Quality #3: Grace

"Grace", a concept I think is a combination of kindness, radical acceptance, and mercy, is, in my opinion, a must-have for outstanding leaders. I've been the recipient of this many times, and as a result, I've learned to give it back. This is a concept that many of us may struggle to understand. What better moment than to illustrate it with a story about how I was the recipient of such grace in the workplace?

"Tammy was one of my direct reports in her early years as a leader in tech. Our company offered the flexibility to work from home decades before it was normalized. At the time, Tammy was balancing her work demands and family commitments. As a young mother, she found being there for her kids completely non-negotiable as she pursued her career aspirations. She made it clear to me that her parenting and caring for her mother meant she would have to leave work earlier on some days. I knew what she was capable of and didn't see these adjustments as problematic for her leadership performance. I am aware that at first, some of her colleagues didn't quite understand her approach. Now, keep in mind this was way before working-from-home was an everyday thing. I'm glad that our *company allowed this flexibility, open mindedness and - shall I say 'kindness' which meant employees could be entrusted with the understanding that as long as they are getting their work done, they don't have to be in the office the full work day. And you know what? Regardless of this flexibility, her performance was still impressive. I think grace goes a long way at creating accommodations that help people flourish in their unique situations."*

- Ronald (Tammy's former boss)

This work-from-home flexibility did not have to exist back then. If this company and my boss had not allowed me the opportunity to work from home, I would have had to find another job that offered its employees unwarranted yet much-needed accommodation. As a result of this grace in my formative leadership phase, I flourished, and my career took off.

Quality #4: Vulnerability

Do you consider vulnerability to be an important quality for effective leaders? Well, in several decades of my leadership, I've come to be convinced that it is certainly one of the qualities that sets apart outstanding leaders. Effective leaders realize that no worker is ever just a "worker". When we step into the workplace, we don't automatically stop being mothers, fathers, partners, daughters, sons, caregivers, survivors, or whatever other role we carry with us in our lives. Every worker attempts to do their job in the workplace with all the other demands humming (hopefully quietly) in their minds. An effective leader knows and acknowledges the multidimensionality of workers. To ignore all these traits and treat a worker as just a worker is not only unrealistic but also highly ineffective. Now, this may sound idealistic, but if you take a moment to consider what leading researchers are doing on the concept of vulnerability, you may come to see my perspective on the matter.

Brene Brown, an acclaimed researcher in the space of vulnerability, connection, and courage, found that participants who experienced a great sense of belonging in their relationships differed from those who felt the exact opposite because of one trait: willingness to be vulnerable[8]. Her research concluded that what leads people to feel a sense of belonging and even love is tied to their willingness to be vulnerable. Conversely, those people who felt overwhelming shame and did not overcome that shame with the courage to express their vulnerability found themselves with a sense of disconnection and even a lack of a sense of belonging.

---

[8] Brown, Brene. "The power of vulnerability". 2010, June. TED Talks. https://www.ted.com/talks/brene_brown_the_power_of_vulnerability

I hope you can see how relevant this trait is when we look at the concept of building teams, even in the workforce. If you and I don't feel like part of the team, then we lack the incentive, maybe even loyalty and ownership, that makes teams sustainable and effective. If you lack that vulnerability, it is easy to pit yourself against your employees. In such a scenario, it is only natural for your team - individually to look out for number one, too.

Expressing or exercising healthy levels of vulnerability may include acknowledging your mistakes to your team when you make them. It may include requesting support or training from your bosses when you know your skills need an upgrade. It may include candid talks with your team during turbulent times and offering them information to ensure you are all aware of a dire situation that affects everyone in the team or even the company. As Brene Brown says, it boils down to the courage to be imperfect.

Quality #5: Authenticity

Another important trait that I believe effective leaders have is "authenticity". I like how Brene Brown describes it. Being "authentic" is essentially letting go of who you think you should be and accepting who you are[9]. Now, I hope no

---

[9] Brown, Brene. "The power of vulnerability". 2010, June. TED Talks. https://www.ted.com/talks/brene_brown_the_power_of_vulnerability

one uses that as an excuse to display unsavory behaviors with the excuse that, "Hey, this is just who I am!". Being authentic does not excuse us from exercising reasonable levels of social graces and general kindness.

Being authentic, however, allows us to take up the space that is rightfully ours. Authenticity allows us to step into any space by acknowledging our unique flavor of being and present our genuine selves with contextualized parts of ourselves. At the same time, I believe the authenticity that extends out from a great leader and great team member is best experienced with genuineness. As authenticity is truly inward-facing for each of us, genuineness is more about how others experience us. Genuineness is defined as an *"intentional apparent attribute of an individual's character which is honestly experienced and thoughtfully shared with others. Genuineness is not spurious or counterfeit; rather it is characterized by realness and sincerity and is independent of hypocrisy.[10]"* I have found that the absence of genuineness often exposed pretentiousness or cockiness, which I've often found unwelcoming and challenging to embrace. When hiring new team members, genuineness is one of the traits I

---

[10] Shaw, Daniel. E. "Genuineness". Living Reference Work Entry. Encyclopedia of Personality and Individual Differences. 2017, April 4.
https://link.springer.com/referenceworkentry/10.1007/978-3-319-28099-8_1475-1#:~:text=Definition,and%20is%20independent%20of%20hypocrisy.

look for in each individual I desire to hire. Likewise, when I want to join a new team, I vet potential new companies and their representatives for a sign of genuine sincerity.

Quality #6: Approachability

Have you ever felt drawn to someone? Has their very presence given you a sense of safety at work or in your personal life? You knew that what you told them at work or in your personal life would be safe, even without explicitly telling them to keep your conversation private. If team members feel apprehensive about engaging with their leaders in the workforce, this creates bottlenecks. These bottlenecks affect your team's performance and desired success. I'm sure you can recall at least one person who could erupt with rage simply by receiving information that they didn't want to hear. Being approachable is more than being welcoming; it's about exuding warmth and willingness to engage with anyone that you interact with. For many leaders, they champion this trait by having an open-door policy, as I do. This may not work for other leaders, since we are all built differently. However, I know that being approachable is rooted in authenticity and a sincere smile. When I asked my network about my strengths as a leader, several people pleasantly surprised me by highlighting my smile as one of their favorite things about interacting with me:

"... Again, I would say leading with a smile: that's very important and unique. I know a lot of leaders and that's a unique quality that I noticed in her. I've seen different kinds of leadership strategies. I've experienced different ways of leading people but, you know, creating a positive vibe, positive energy with a smile is, I think a unique characteristic. I think though, people who do serve others with a smile are so used to it that they don't realize how unique it is especially as leaders. ..."

- Abdul

When I reflect on great leaders I've known, their defaulting towards **"service with a smile"** is a simple but noteworthy aspect of what contributed to them being outstanding.

Quality #7: Credibility

Here's the trick, though: vulnerability and authenticity can be dangerous for you and even your team if you lack credibility. Credibility means "your ability to be believable or worthy of trust[11]". It is trustworthiness and competence

---

[11] Dictionary.com. "Credibility". 2023.
https://www.dictionary.com/browse/credibility

combined. If you know me or have ever spoken to anyone who's worked with me, you'll note that many people would share something about my fun and warm side. These attributes are authentic to me. I approach any space I go into with an appropriate level of authenticity and sometimes vulnerability. For many years, I have effectively taken this approach in spaces not known for fun or even warmth. Yet, I have been effective. How, you may wonder? Because my fun and empathy are backed up by competence and credibility. I've learned that if you can deliver, people are far more accommodating or accepting of your authenticity and vulnerability.

People realize and respect your unique approach when you meet deadlines, effectively accomplish goals, and consistently show up. For over 30 years, I've experienced people who would never dream of leading like me acknowledging the effectiveness of my unique approach and sometimes even embracing it for themselves.

The bottom line is you've got to perform effectively. That effective performance gives you leverage to operate with authenticity and vulnerability, even in worlds where many of us don't dare to "come as ourselves".

Quality #8: Loyalty

All leaders want loyal teams. From that vantage point,

it's easy to forget that the people in our teams also desire and need our loyalty. At the face value, it's a reasonable summation. But how many times have you heard of employees terrified of being thrown under the proverbial bus by their bosses that they know aren't looking out for them?

A great leader ensures they offer the team they hire the same level of loyalty that they expect from them. This may look like standing up to top management to protect a team from negative repercussions that are unfair or untimely. Sometimes, this may look like the leader absorbing the brunt force of a negative impact while encouraging the team to perform at their ultimate best.

Quality #9: Respect

Focusing on people's ranking in an organization may lead us to believe that not everyone is worth respect. Maybe you've seen it yourself and live to tell the tale. Again, as with loyalty, great leaders have a level of respect for everyone, including members of their team. I'm sure you've been in spaces where you felt disrespected or undervalued. Even if a word to that effect is not said, I'm sure you could sense it.

When we understand that all human beings are equal and worthy of respect, it is easy to give that respect to everyone you interact with in your work experience, including people who report to you.

Quality #10: Inspiration

Think about any great leader in your life that you admire. I'm willing to bet that they could inspire or motivate you. Maybe it wasn't because of their rhetoric, poetic or riveting wordsmithing. Perhaps it was simply how they carried themselves despite incredible odds. Was it because they stood up for you and your team even when it was clear their bosses were exerting enormous pressure on them, and you knew it took everything they were to show up every day at their best? Or perhaps it is because they modeled the lifestyle you still aspired to achieve. I don't know what they did to inspire or motivate you, but you do. And that ingredient is important for you to possess as you exercise your leadership capabilities.

Quality #11: Creativity

A famous quote attributed to Albert Einstein sums this trait up nicely: "Creativity is intelligence having fun[12]". I love using creativity to drive home points I want my team to pay special attention to. From gifting my team vials of 'pixie

---

[12] Goodreads. "Creativity is intelligence having fun."

— Albert Einstein". Quotable Quote. n.d.
https://www.goodreads.com/quotes/37706-creativity-is-intelligence-having-fun

dust' to sending them 'magic wands', to motivational quotes reflective of the collective experience our team may be going through at that time of the month, to off-the-clock sessions where we collectively get to reset, recalibrate and reconnect in a low-pressure setting every month. These are areas of my leadership I was grateful to display my creativity.

Now, you may find my approach not authentic, and that's okay. Creativity doesn't have to be as expressive or unique as my approach. However, I do believe it is a crucial trait to have as a leader. It just may look a bit different coming from you. Like one creative individual once said, "You don't have to be 'a creative' to be creative[13]". In its simplest form, creativity is the result of conflicting ideas[14]. Trying new ideas, activities, or approaches to help your team or yourself perform better is an expression of creativity.

Quality #12: Generosity

If you find that you have "a willingness to give help or

---

[13] Wichita State University. Software Available for Use. n.d.
https://www.wichita.edu/services/mrc/OIR/Creative/1Design/design-software.php

[14] Goodreads. "Creativity comes from a conflict of ideas"

— Donatella Versace". Goodreads. n.d.
https://www.goodreads.com/quotes/663215-creativity-comes-from-a-conflict-of-ideas

support, esp. more than is usual or expected[15]" then you have another important quality for being a great leader - generosity. Though generosity is intuitive to me, I guess somewhere down the line I learned how gratifying it was to show others through tokens of my expression that I valued them as individuals and that I was invested in their presence in my teams and life. It's amazing what a small and thoughtful gift can do to touch another person's heart. As my team's well-being is important to me, sometimes I would fund experiences I wanted us to have together, especially the off-the-clock sessions I mentioned as we discussed "Creativity". We called those "Decompression Sessions" and these would sometimes mean we all get 1 and a half hour for personal time once a month or spend time together having fun or relaxing. This could be going for breakfast, bowling, or snacks and drinks during that block of time. It was my pleasure to offer these experiences to my team and to engage with them in a manner that reaffirmed to them the value I placed in them as human beings that aren't just a number on payroll.

Quality #13: Transparency

Have you ever found yourself in a situation where

---

[15] Cambridge Dictionary. "Generosity". English. Cambridge Dictionary. n.d. https://dictionary.cambridge.org/dictionary/english/generosity

your career was at stake, and you didn't know what was coming next? Information trickling down from their bosses was only enough to have you know that job cuts and other unpleasant things were imminent. This information was so sparse that you didn't know what to do other than brace yourself for whatever would unfold. Well, you're not alone. I've noticed one outstanding quality of leaders that helps teams overcome turbulent times in the workplace: transparency. When a boss can tell you, "Hey, I hate to tell you this, but the company is being bought out, and some of us may need to start getting our resumes in order", it's hard to hear. But it is also actionable and supportive of your next move. This ability helps leaders create a sense of safety for teams, even in uncomfortable and difficult times. No one likes to have to make decisions when they feel uninformed. As such, a leader who exercises a healthy level of transparency can create an enabling environment just by offering people actionable information.

Quality #14: Resilience

It's never a smooth journey. If you look at the stories of some of the world's most impactful leaders across fields, we'll see that most of them experienced seemingly insurmountable odds. Some of the tough times and unfortunate events that become part of their lives are things none of us would wish upon our worst enemies. Yet there they were, still leading teams to greatness or simply getting them through some of the toughest times their teams could ever live to see. And that's all thanks to "resilience". You can be celebrated at work one day and denigrated or castigated the next. You can be the star player, and sooner than you know it, you will be the pariah in the eyes of people who fail to see your true worth. It takes resilience to stand firm and confident in who you are whilst still acknowledging that "this too shall pass".

Resilience is strongly linked to the next trait - adaptability. In fast-paced societies, there can be moments, months, and even whole seasons where you must keep rolling with the punches until you get to the other side. A leader without resilience can't successfully navigate themselves to the other side of this.

Quality #15: Adaptability

Being able to see change coming and take the appropriate action keeps you moving forward. This trait is fundamental when it comes to navigating transformational change. If you are adaptable, you are not stuck thinking about "how we did things yesterday" or "this worked just fine". Adaptable leaders, acknowledge those facts of what worked yesterday and embrace the need to accept that yesterday (for all intents and purposes) is irrevocably gone.

And all we have is the future that lies before us, demanding we choose one of two options: adapt or die.

An adaptive leader is a responsive leader. A leader who takes thoughtful steps that are controlled and calculated. It is impossible to lead transformational change if you lack adaptability.

Quality #16: Proactivity

As I studied my favorite leaders, I noticed that they all displayed certain levels of proactivity. You see them taking charge in various ways. Now, I don't mean they went off and micromanaged their teams. But I do mean they didn't sit down and wait for events to happen to them. Instead, they constantly exercised their sense of personal power and accountability. They acknowledged what was in their zone of influence and what they could control. Then they took all the steps they could reasonably take to ensure success whilst accepting what they couldn't control.

Quality #17: Integrity

I mentioned how credibility is a crucial quality the best leaders have. I also added how trustworthiness is a component of that credibility. However, trustworthiness is also a part of integrity. When we know that a leader is credible and has integrity, we get to enjoy a sense of safety. You know that they are who they say they are. You also know that when push comes to shove, they won't shove you under the bus or let you take a hit for something they know they are ultimately responsible for. That doesn't mean a great leader doesn't hold their teams accountable. On the contrary, great leaders expect their teams to be worthy of any trust they are given.

Quality #18: Active Listener (Effective Communicator)

Like me, you are probably already sold on the importance of effective communication. Have you ever noticed how smoothly everything runs in a system where everyone communicates as and when expected? How about the annoyance of thinking you effectively articulated a point, only to find that the other party hadn't heard what you said or at least didn't care to listen?

Great leaders are capable of distilling complex ideas into digestible and simple concepts. They take up the role of 'translator' as they promptly present their bosses and team with actionable information.

From my experience, one of the best qualities you can have - especially in communication- is being an active listener. As leadership expert Stephen R. Covey once said, "The Biggest communication problem is we don't listen to understand. We listen to reply".[16] It's not enough to parrot back to someone what they just told you. We all appreciate when we interact with someone and feel not only heard but felt and understood. That's what you give to your team when you actively listen and respond appropriately to the exchange. That emotional resonance can not be faked. I even believe that without active listening, you can not build trust with your team, ultimately an authentic or sustainable connection with them, or as bonds to hold the team together.

People can sense that they are tolerated, ignored, or manipulated. When you want to be an effective leader, there's no room for that. The role demands your stepping up and learning to be present with those you interact with as a leader.

Quality #19: Committed Learner

There is always going to be something you don't know. No matter how up the leadership ladder you climb. The best leaders I've interacted with make efforts to stay up-to-date and informed. They don't sit on their laurels and

---

[16] Buckenmaier, Chester III. MD. "The biggest communication problem is we don't listen to understand; we listen to reply. - Stephen R. Covey." 2022, January 10. "https://www.usmedicine.com/editor-in-chief/the-biggest-communication-problem-is-we-dont-listen-to-understand-we-listen-to-reply/

survey the expanse of their zone of influence. No, these leaders stay on top of trends. They are active in networks and peer groups. They contribute to their industries in ways that seem right for them, and they are not afraid to take a certification, executive training program, or course to upgrade their skills. In fields like technology, it may be obvious why staying on top of advancements is crucial. After all, how can you make effective decisions in an evolving global landscape when you lack the necessary information?

Quality #20: Strategic Thinker

When I look at the most impactful leaders I know, among the many qualities they share, being a strategic thinker is right up there. A leader needs to be able to see the forest from the trees. I've noticed that some of the most brilliant leaders, especially those coming from a strong technical background, may find this integrally challenging. It can be hard to separate yourself from the details because of years of training where focusing on minutiae was not only helpful but crucial for great performance in their previous roles, especially in technical roles. However, at some point, a leader realizes it is no longer effective for the whole team's optimal performance to be so deeply in the details. There are simply not enough hours in the day to operate in that way successfully and sustainably.

Now, I'm not just talking about micromanagement, which is ineffective for building robust teams. I am talking about a lifestyle of focusing "on the trees". This could look like insisting on troubleshooting ourselves when we have a team that exists to do that for the organization. It could also look like attending meetings that you could delegate to your capable reports. I'm talking about creating designs or code, documents, and whatever else that someone in your organization is capable of doing well and has the time and job responsibility to effectively execute. Being a strategic thinker does not mean you never look at the trees. When you must, you have to take a moment to focus on the trees. Roll up your sleeves and sort out a situation that demands your attention. However, it should be more the exception than the rule. Being a strategic, political, or holistic thinker also helps you navigate how to have the desired results with the variables unique to your situation.

Being a strategic thinker looks like an uncanny ability to connect all the pieces of the puzzle even before you have them all on the table. It can also look like connecting ideas, processes, and people to get the results you need.

Quality #21: Effective Delegator

I kind of hinted at this quality when I talked about a "strategic perspective" earlier in this list of important leadership qualities. However, it is worth taking a moment and discussing this matter further in detail. From my observation, great leaders are effective at hiring great talent and empowering them to fully embody their selected roles. These leaders are also skilled at repositioning team members who aren't in optimal roles and helping them navigate toward their best fits, whether inside the existing time or outside of it. It's pretty hard to be an effective leader when you feel the need to do everything. In addition, how do we help talented or skilled employees rise in leadership if we don't entrust them with responsibilities that allow them to showcase what they are made of?

It's the mark of a great leader when they take the ego out of their leadership efforts and structure team dynamics that allow their team and the organization to chug along successfully, even if they are not there at all. If you ask me, one of the best signs of successful leadership is when a leader exits an organization and everything they worked towards continues to work without things falling apart. People who don't see the "before and after" of such efforts often don't have the privilege of seeing just how much of an impact a leader who empowers their teams can make. One of the successes I am most proud of is how every team I built and eventually exited managed to make great strides, even after I was long gone.

Quality #22: Decisiveness

Do you think great leaders only make good decisions? We both probably know that's not the case. Perfection is impossible. All the effective leaders I've known over the years can make informed decisions with enough partial information. Sometimes, you need 100% of the information to make critical decisions. Often, though, you don't. You need enough data to analyze to make an informed decision. And sometimes enough data is 70 or 80%. And oftentimes, the decisions an effective leader makes with this amount of data are enough. Now, mistakes may happen, but a great leader understands how to weigh and balance the concepts of risk and reward and arrive at a healthy and acceptable balance.

Quality #23: Hardworking Spirit

Usually, when we talk about a "hardworking spirit", we mean the efforts we exert physically. I've noticed that the best leaders, though, often work hard in ways you may not even notice. Developing more empathy, grace, self-control, transparency, and proactivity is not easy. When you feel safe doing everything yourself, getting someone else to take on the responsibility is unpleasant, regardless of how capable they are. If you aren't used to a lifestyle of integrity, trying to operate in that paradigm is formidable. Great leaders may not be breaking a sweat when they respond with restraint and grace to overt disrespect. However, I bet they deploy significant effort not to lose themselves in a "make-or-break" moment with all the self-control they can muster. All of this is work, hard work, until it becomes second nature. Once that quality becomes part of who you are and your psyche, you may not even remember how you operated any other way.

Quality #24: Jointly Accountability

"Julia is the reason that we failed to meet our targets this month!". "If only the group I assigned this responsibility had done their job, we would have succeeded". Assigning blame is easy and often even justified. Candidates for carrying blame are endless. We also know assigning blame is hardly ever productive, even though all team members have responsibilities they are wholly responsible for. But when it comes to leadership, no matter what Jack or Jill did, the fact is that bad results are you and your team's collective outcome. You don't get to marinate in the glory of your team's success whilst pointing the spotlight elsewhere when your team's performance is not as you'd hoped. If you believe success is a team effort - which it is, then it's logical and wise to operate with the understanding that failure is just the same. Like Rudyard Kipling said, "If you can meet with triumph and disaster... And treat those two impostors just the same[17]". The leaders I admire the most understand this concept of joint accountability. Any win is a "we" thing, And so is any loss.

Quality #25: Self-control (Breathe)

We've all flown off the handle at least once. Maybe not in the workplace. Maybe at home or on the way to work, running late and stuck in ridiculous traffic. Some of us take our rage to our friends, who offer themselves as mutual sounding boards and buffers to process intense emotions so those emotions don't become actions that end up causing social friction wherever we experience this turmoil.

Whatever the case, modern-day life offers a plethora of opportunities to exercise self-control. Perhaps more opportunities than most of us would choose, given the chance. Leaders capable of reigning in their strong negative emotions have incredible potential for growth and positive impact. It's amazing how one word, a steely glance, a look of disdain, or an air of resolute discard can have on members of your team. You and I know how hard it is to take the high ground when we would rather just let an adversary have it. And that is why leaders who have harnessed self-control are exceptional. The funny thing is, anyone willing can grow and

---

[17] Poets.org. "If - Rudyard Kipling" . Poems. (n.d.). https://poets.org/poem/if

exercise more self-control. It can look like taking a moment to pause and breathe before you take any action. Science tells us that pausing for just six seconds[18] can give our nervous systems the chance to stop automatically reacting to a conscious and metered response. Every single time I've taken a moment to consciously pause and just breathe has helped me countless times in stressful and charged moments when strong emotions could have gotten the best of me.

Your Personal Life

Now that we've looked at the great qualities of a leader, let's circle back to another factor that can affect your ability to be a great leader. One of these additional factors is your personal life. Our personal lives, regardless of them being personal, are factors that affect our effectiveness. Your personal life is an aspect that influences your success as a leader and impacts your team's success as a whole. We don't operate in vacuums.

This is a challenging subject for me to share in a book

---

[18] Anderson, Ase. "The Six Second Rule that Changes Everything". Social Etiquette. 2020, July 31. https://thebritishschoolofexcellence.com/social-etiquette/the-6-second-rule-that-changes-everything/#:~:text=Taking%20a%206%2Dsecond%20pause,or%20appropriate%20way%20to%20act.

about team building, but I would be doing many of you a disservice if I omitted it. The very challenges I faced across my leadership journey are the ones you may face at this very moment. You are trying to get that promotion while you care for a struggling loved one. You're trying to meet looming deadlines whilst being a single parent. You're trying to invest in your leadership capabilities, yet you're exhausted, never seem to have any time, and are doubting your capability to do it all in this season of your life. You want to get more responsibilities in your roles, but the negative criticisms are bearing down on you so hard. You're afraid. Sometimes you even wonder if the naysayers could be right.

But I have very good news for you: as someone who's been a leader in corporate America for over 3 decades, I've got to tell you: you can survive setbacks at work. You can navigate through sabotage. You can be a single mom and a corporate key player. You can excel whilst healing a broken heart in your personal life. You can rise in male-dominated industries and allow yourself to be seen as the equal that you are. You can figure out how to take care of your aging parents and figure out how to create more impact in the workforce as authentically as possible. And what's more, you can do this again and again... and again. As someone who navigated personal tragedies and those of loved ones many times over, I know from first-hand experience, it is possible to experience life in its potency and not let it shut you down. In the chapter on Self-care, I'll take a moment to share specific examples from my own life.

Building Effective Leadership Qualities

Being an effective leader and acquiring the qualities above is a journey. You can help yourself along the way through self-assessment, 360 feedback, receiving coaching, and your networking efforts.

Self-Assessment

Having taken time to look at the qualities of a great leader, I hope you took a moment to honestly and compassionately look inward. My simple rule for identifying which areas to work on beyond listening to 360 Feedback is a combination of self-reflection, acceptance, and honesty. You need to identify your internal resistance. When I reflect on my leadership qualities, and something about me bugs me, I know I have some work to do. Perhaps checking in and identifying that sense within yourself can guide your leadership self-improvement efforts. I've noticed, though, that it's impossible to do without a level of humility and self-awareness.

360 - Degree Feedback

As I stated in the first quality, we need a healthy level of self-awareness to be great leaders; part of that involves understanding how others view us. Yes, I know this can be a brutal endeavor. But when you have fair people to offer you feedback, those people and their feedback are worth more than their weight in gold. If you are not familiar with the term, "360-feedback" is where you get evaluated multi-directionally. That means not just your boss but your peers, customers, and reportees.

360 feedback is important as it offers you a more accurate or even holistic appraisal of how you're doing as a leader. This approach offers you a fair and consistent assessment of your leadership performance and its perception from everyone around you.

Networking

Early in my leadership career, I made sure to join peer groups. Networking and rubbing shoulders with the best in the industry opened me up to a world of opportunity. To this day, I remain actively involved in networking.

You are probably aware of several theories about the impact that social connections may have on several areas of your life. Actively getting involved and reaching out could be the one action that stands between you and your next leadership role. Take a moment to consider the concept of

"Six Degrees of Separation[19]". With "Six Degrees of Separation", we know there are probably just six people between the person who would happily hire us. Networking is your secret tool in your arsenal because it may open you up to people and resources you need, such as role models, mentors, diversity of perspectives, and growth opportunities. Additionally, it allows you to flex your emotional intelligence and communication skills while navigating your way around.

Coaching

Do all great leaders need coaches, mentors, or advisors? I certainly don't know the answer to that, but I'll tell you one thing: all great leaders I know have had someone or several people who've offered them that level of support. Some have executive coaches, and others have trusted colleagues, mentors, and advisors who give them perspective, knowledge, and insights that they sometimes can't see by themselves. Heck, at various times in my career, I've had all three: executive coaches, mentors, and trusted colleagues/ advisors. I am certain that their impact on my life has contributed to who I am as a leader in more ways than one.

---

[19] Morse, Gardiner. "The Science Behind Six Degrees

by Gardiner Morse". Innovation. The Harvard Business Review. 2003, February. https://hbr.org/2003/02/the-science-behind-six-degrees

What I've learned in my career is that you never truly arrive. Being a great leader involves continuous committed improvement. Even if you feel you've mastered one area, you may discover that another aspect could do with attention, effort, and improvement.

The Team

Since we've finished looking inward, let's now look outward. Great leaders know that it is never about the leader. It's about the team. Several dynamics are directly about team members or directly impact any team. These dynamics include the qualities of a team, diversity, equity, equality, inclusion, and neurodiversity. We will take a moment to shed light on each of these. We will conclude this section by exploring what it looks like to understand your team. However, firstly, let's agree on what a team is and take a moment to look at the qualities that make a great team.

Simply put, a team is a group of people, often with defined roles, working together to achieve one agreed-upon vision. You've probably heard the saying by Dr. John Maxwell, "Teamwork makes the dream work[20]". Most of us

---

[20] Weber, John Leo. "Best Teamwork Quotes: 35 Motivational Quotes for Teams". Project Manager. 2023, January 20.
https://www.projectmanager.com/blog/teamwork-quotes-25-best-inspirational-

have heard such sayings so much that they have since lost their meaning for us. I encourage you to consider all the things you've achieved in your life. How many of those things did you manage to do on your own? If you earned a certification, I bet you had a decent teacher. Did you exceed your sales targets? I bet you had several people on your team helping to make that happen. Do you have mentors or even children who are doing a great job? It's not just genes or your influence that helped shape them into who they are today. An element of teamwork led to stepping into that joint vision. Now, let's talk about the qualities of great teams.

Qualities of a Great Team

From my experience, all 25 qualities I've presented to you as qualities of a great leader are inherently the qualities that great teams have. I would encourage you to go back to that list and evaluate your team for the presence of these qualities. If you find opportunities for improvement, I invite you to consider what steps you can take to start nurturing these qualities in your team members. What I believe never fails is this: when a leader embodies certain qualities and consistently exhibits them, it offers their team an undeniable challenge to step up and attempt to grow in those areas as well.

---

quotes-working-together

Understanding Your Team

Knowing yourself is only the first step in creating a great team. The next step is understanding your team. You could have a great person in the wrong role. Taking time to get to know what everyone in your team brings to the table is vital. You've probably seen the trouble of people who don't fit in a team. But that's not the only concern.

You can have amazing folks underperforming and hating their jobs simply because they are in the wrong roles or need support to perform better but aren't given any paths to navigate that kind of improvement. I've seen firsthand how people blossom when you respond to shifting them into roles that align with their capabilities, interests, and career goals.

When they blossom, the team's overall performance improves, even if that sometimes means helping them prepare for their exit from their existing team into another part of the organization or another organization entirely.

Diversity, Equity / Equality, and Inclusion

The best leaders I ever met taught me that our differences are what make our organization complete and ultimately successful. However, they also taught me that we have to be deliberate about supporting the safety of what makes us unique and ensuring everyone gets a seat at the table and enough resources proportional to their needs to be successful in whatever roles they are assigned. Though these leaders know that the core of what makes a human being is the same, they know that's not enough to reach a person as an individual. People want to know that their differences are seen, accepted, welcomed, and accommodated. For that reason, taking time to survey the landscape of diversity, equity/equality, and inclusion in the workforce is more than something the human resources department is responsible for alone. These aspects are more than fashionable or politically correct perspectives to have about humanity to show how progressive we are. These concepts are the bare minimum of operating with the most important trait of great leaders: empathy. Let's look at each a little closer.

Diversity

If you know me, you know that my teams are often quite diverse. My team members, business partners, and even friends from all over the world have shared their uniqueness, expanding my worldview. I've worked with folks of different ages, genders, races, ethnicities, sexual orientations, religions, nationalities, cultures, intellectual capacities, personalities, and professional backgrounds. I have enjoyed, been enriched, led, and learned from all types of people. This diversity has brought with it increased creativity, a global perspective, and innovation.

Embracing diversity requires the bare minimum of mutual respect. When my Indian reports wish me a "Merry Christmas" or "Happy Thanksgiving" and I wish them a "Blessed Diwali" for those who are Hindu or "Eid Mubarak!" for those who are Muslim, this small gesture gives them a glimpse at my desire to acknowledge, embrace and celebrate our differences.

Neurodivergence

Though neurodivergence is certainly another facet of diversity, I found it important to separate and highlight it here. We are fortunate to live in a time when we know about neurodivergence. Whether it's ADHD, Bipolar, the Autism Spectrum, or a whole lot of other labels that exist to represent these differences, we are now in a better time than ever to approach each other with a level of grace in light of these differences. Not so long ago, people would just consider someone "higher-active", "moody" or even unreliable when there is so much more going on underneath the surface. As a leader, I've had to work with people who are either diagnosed with certain conditions or suspect they may have something impacting how they appear in the world. Often, these conditions can be a sensitive matter for anyone to discuss. That's why leaders must lead with integrity and compassion. Our teams need to know that they can trust us to handle their personal information with grace and discretion as they figure out any adjustments they may need to make in their careers for their success and, ultimately, that of the team.

Thankfully, many workplaces make accommodations for our differences in brain function, though there is still an opportunity for more to be done. This is also why I enjoy sitting with my team members and asking how they are doing and how I can get out of their way so that they can do their jobs effectively.

Equity and Equality

As I'm sure you know, equality is the state of being equal[21]. With the disparities that exist in the world, treating each other equally is simply not enough. Our differences affect our life experiences and even our success in the workforce.

When we encounter circumstances that render "equality" insufficient, " equity " must be applied. "Equity", is about fairness. It is about treating people fairly in light of their differences, especially as it pertains to access and needs "[22]". The illustrations below help explain the differences

EQUALITY VERSUS EQUITY

In the first image, it is assumed that everyone will benefit from the same supports. They are being treated equally.

In the second image, individuals are given different supports to make it possible for them to have equal access to the game. They are being treated equitably.

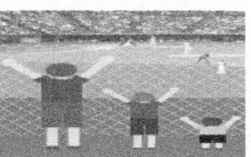
In the third image, all three can see the game without any supports or accommodations because the cause of the inequity was addressed. The systemic barrier has been removed.

further.

23

---

[21] Merriam-Webster. (n.d.). Equality. In Merriam-Webster.com dictionary. Retrieved September 14, 2023, from https://www.merriam-webster.com/dictionary/equality

[22] Human Rights Careers. "What is Social Equity?". (n.d.). Human Rights Careers. https://www.humanrightscareers.com/issues/what-is-social-equity

[23] Diffen. "Equality vs. Equity". Diffen. https://www.diffen.com/difference/Equality-

Inclusion

From a social responsibility perspective, the dictionary defines "inclusion" as "the act of allowing many different types of people to do something and treating them fairly and equally[24]". I know many of us have had our own experiences - both positive and negative - when it comes to inclusion. With the pop-culture popularity of the term, many organizations rush to implement policies and integrate elements of inclusion without pausing to assess whether their implicit culture truly matches their explicit culture. Perhaps you've seen it yourself: an organization talks about inclusion or diversity, and on the ground, there seems to be no direct access to enjoy that inclusion. We all know inclusion can't only be on paper. Inclusion is something we see and even feel in terms of how accommodating and welcoming of our differences as a leader, team, and organization is.

The Organization

Perhaps you've heard the phrase, "People don't leave bad Jobs, they leave bad bosses[25]". Whether or not we think

---

vs-Equity

[24] Cambridge Dictionary. "Inclusion". (n.d.).
https://dictionary.cambridge.org/us/dictionary/english/inclusion

[25] Kelly, Jack. "People Don't Leave Bad Jobs, They Leave Bad Bosses: Here's How

it's become a cliche, the truth is that an organization filled with good leaders creates an environment that very few people ever want to leave. This combined atmosphere with the team and the organization's processes form an organization. This "lifestyle" everyone experiences inside or outside the company is essentially the organization's culture. Let's take a moment to discuss this culture further.

Organizational Culture

If you've ever had the experience of working at a company with great company culture and another with poor company culture, I bet the contrast alone is a good reminder of why it's important to understand the company culture, how you fit or can operate within it and how it will affect the success of your team. When making the move to join a new team, it's worth taking a moment to assess whether the values, beliefs, attitudes, and practices that the company presents are actually what the organization "lives". Apart from asking questions in your interviews that point to the answers you seek, ask former or current employees what their experiences were or are like. Get as much objective

---

To Be A Better Manager To Maintain And Motivate Your Team". Editor's Pick. Forbes. 2019, November 21.
https://www.forbes.com/sites/jackkelly/2019/11/22/people-dont-leave-bad-jobs-they-leave-bad-bosses-heres-how-to-be-a-better-manager-to-maintain-and-motivate-your-team/?sh=24a9a64922b9

information as possible and assess subjective responses as diligently as possible. Remember the impact a poor work experience can have beyond the financial incentive or social clout a role or opportunity may present.

One tricky scenario is when the explicit culture of an organization is misaligned with its implicit culture. Explicit culture is the culture that we can observe socially without analyzing nuances[26]. Explicit culture guides our behavior and helps us feel accepted. We wear business attire to work, not only because it's in the company guidelines but because it's what we know to wear in that specific context. We normally don't sing in the office, but when there's a birthday cake present, the context changes, and we all know what to do.

"Implicit culture," on the other hand, is the culture of unspoken and nuanced patterns of behavior in our societies that we may not all be consciously aware of[27]. It's the "good ole' boy" clubs that still thrive in workforces around the

---

[26] Open Education Sociology Dictionary. "Explicit Culture". (n.d.). https://sociologydictionary.org/explicit-culture

[27] Szalay, Lorand. B. Maday, Bela. C. "Implicit Culture and Psychoculture Distance". 1983, March. AntrhoSource. https://anthrosource.onlinelibrary.wiley.com/doi/abs/10.1525/aa.1983.85.1.02a00070

world. The unconscious biases may underpin certain decisions we make as leaders. The good news is that once we drive awareness to unhealthy elements of implicit culture and create opportunities for change, that light can help us create a more equitable society. Consider pay parity as one aspect of implicit culture that was moved into the spotlight. We may not have reached equal pay for all, but at least conscious efforts are being made towards it.

Business / Market Forces

As much as many of us wish being a leader only encompassed you and your team's scope of control, the reality is there are so many forces - business or market forces that affect the success of any team. These include mergers, acquisitions, privatization, initial public offerings (IPOs), health or natural disasters, advancement in technology, industry trends, and even politics.

Mergers, Acquisitions, and Divestitures

I've had the experience of working in two companies that got bought out by larger corporations. This is an experience that can challenge even the most stoic leaders. When you're scared, your bosses are scared, and no one knows what's coming next, it can be very hard to stand in front of your team, eager - not only for information but reassurance. Will they still have their jobs next month?

Should they be worried? Is there anything that they can do to ensure they come out on top? These are all questions you end up fielding as you struggle to find the same answers for yourself. Worse, you must do this while ensuring your team maintains optimal performance. This is quite tricky because this air of uncertainty is not very motivational. I always tell my team to keep their resumes up to date. This is advice I apply for myself, too, because the fact of the matter is, often these types of changes come unannounced. Since you can't do anything to stop such changes, the best thing you can do for yourself as a leader and for your team is to ensure you, and they are prepared for any eventuality.

Unprecedented Events

We all saw the impact that the CoronaVirus Pandemic had on a global scale. This unprecedented mass even changed the shape of business globally almost in the blink of an eye. It's important to remember that just as the pandemic materialized from thin air (excuse the pun), other undesirable events came too. These forces impacting the work our teams put out in the world demand our attention and effective navigation. During the pandemic, many of us learned how to keep working despite lockdowns and changes in how we work. We had to learn to work from home. We had to learn better time-management and we had to learn that being in an office didn't equate to actually working. Even as the world attempts to switch back to something akin to "normal", natural disasters and mass concerns impact how we show up at work. From my experience, the only way to ensure we come out on the other side of unprecedented events like the pandemic is by applying innovation and letting go of what we consider "the way we do things". As tedious as endless virtual meetings can be, it's worth appreciating that we have these innovative alternatives to avoid a full shutdown. After all, for many of us, a full shutdown would translate into lost jobs and the inability to find other opportunities in the saturated job market.

Advancement in Technology

I hinted at Zoom and other online virtual meeting platforms that keep us connected and collaborating even during the worst of times. Such innovative solutions, including advances in artificial intelligence, cybersecurity, and financial services, are among many other advances in technology that are changing the way we live and work. In my field- cybersecurity - advancement is neverending. What worked before may become obsolete in a matter of weeks or even months. New threats or opportunities drive the need for more technology applications. Without these continuous advancements, which may sometimes feel like hassles or inconveniences, many of us would be in danger of threats that we are unaware of. From identity theft and hacking leading to loss of income and a negative impact on reputation and credibility, advancing technology helps protect us from what we don't want to be exposed to. As with the benefits that technology offered us during the height of the pandemic, it's worth keeping in mind how beneficial tech can be to growing and sustaining the teams we build.

Industry Trends

I mentioned artificial intelligence as one area of advancing technology that we both probably know. With the growing usage of such technology, new trends pop up. When people hire large teams of experts, firms may choose to cut down on the size of their teams and let technology do the heavy lifting whilst we humans man the machines. As much as many of us may wish to keep our heads buried in the sand, this trend by employers is likely to continue to grow. It's our job to figure out how to make these trends work for us as individuals, leaders, and members of organizations.

Politics

Governance has a huge impact on how we work, as I'm sure you know. New policies are springing up everywhere, especially where technology forces change.

Sometimes it takes time for policies to be created and deployed, but sure enough, they will come. As a leader, you must stay abreast of any laws, policies, or information pertaining to you, your team, and the whole organization.

My Message to You

In this chapter, we touched on the dynamics that can influence the success of your team. These dynamics included both external and internal forces. We began by discussing what a leader is and how a great leader differs from a manager. We then looked at the qualities of great leaders. As no one ever truly arrives, we took a moment to look at the efforts you can make to develop your leadership acumen capabilities further. Having taken a hard look at ourselves as leaders, we focused on the external forces that impact the success of teams, such as market forces, diversity, equity, equality, inclusion, other team dynamics, and lastly, the leader's personal life.

As we conclude this chapter, let me leave you with this: Though you can not control many of these forces that impact your team's performance, it is your responsibility to be aware of these dynamics and prepare your team for success amidst them.

We've talked about leadership, the team, and the

organization as three things that can make or break you as a leader. In chapter two, we change the focus. In chapter two, we focus on the type of people, the skill sets required, and how to maximize the performance of a great team. Let's jump into it.

Chapter 2

Getting The Right People on Your Bus

"First who, then what?" - *Jim Collins*[28]

You may recognize this from a key phrase coined by Jim Collins in his book titled "Good to Great" as "getting the right people on the bus". If you can get the right people on your team, you are one step closer to guaranteeing your team's success. I have a process that has worked well for me over the past three decades, and I would like to share it with you in this chapter. I could just go ahead and start explaining either process, but I think that's not the best place to start. As a team leader, you are a part of that team. So, I'll start with you.

---

[28]Collins, J. Good to great: Why some companies make the leap and others don't. 2001. Harper Business.

For you to lead it, you have to decide to join it. For logical reasons, we need to begin this conversation there. You have to choose the organization you work for wisely for many reasons, including the fact that there are certainly some benefits and constraints depending on what you end up selecting. So, let's start there: how you choose where you want to lead.

Choosing Where to Serve (The Leader)

When I evaluate new job opportunities, I begin with much self-reflection. You want to make sure you choose a workplace that sees value in you beyond your technical abilities. You want a workplace in which their company culture and you are a fit. It is not an ideal scenario to find yourself in an office that requires you to pretend to be who you aren't. In such a case, that is not a sustainable scenario for either you or the organization.

Why Join a Team

Sometimes, I am drawn to a job opportunity because the culture fit is exactly what I am looking for, and they offer me a challenge that I can't seem to find anywhere else. Money is not the number one deciding factor for me.

Apart from the elements of a job offer that pique my interest, feeling comfortable is paramount. It's about feeling comfortable with the people in the organization, the job description I'll fit, the hiring process, and the organization's culture.

When it comes to the people in the organization, I pay attention to the character of the individuals I interface with. In particular, those that I will be reporting to. If I sense a level of cockiness or ego that does not resonate with what I am about, I consider it a red flag. I am drawn to people and environments that allow authenticity and genuineness. Pretense is a complete put-off.

You may have your own set of reasons why you decide to join a given team. Be true to yourself and what's important to you. What I do think is important for everyone is to find a safe work environment. If you sense hostility or dysfunction right off the bat, that's a sure indicator - before you sign a contract – that you may be likely to experience that on an ongoing basis. And then the question becomes: is that the work experience you would like for yourself indefinitely? Is it worth whatever financial compensation you receive in turn? Is it worth your mental health and emotional wellbeing? Each of us is responsible for coming to our own conclusions, which will vary.

Taking Up a Challenge

Sometimes, you might spot these red flags, but feel

confident you can turn this team around and function well. This requires a level of self-awareness about how willing or committed you are to take up this challenge and whether you have it in you to be integral to a turnaround. If you decide to take up such a challenge, prepare yourself for whatever may come along. Ensure you build into your plan a way to mitigate the factors you foresaw.

I bet you've seen a job or two that you felt you could successfully take on but noticed you didn't fit the job description to a T. You know what? That's okay. Go ahead and submit your application. Sometimes organizations are willing to overlook that, hoping you will step up and learn what you lack. Don't self-disqualify yourself.

Let me take a moment to discuss the maturity of a company's interview process. You want to pay attention to how thorough their interview process is. If their process is not thorough, it is a good indicator that the organization you are considering joining may not be as mature as you would desire.

Sometimes an organization that has an enormous opportunity to grow may give you a job offer and your experience with their hiring process is less than ideal. If you find yourself still interested, make sure you understand the job description, as you would in any case, but also take the initiative to request clarity where you find none was provided.

At Your Interview

When you find yourself in the interview room, I want you to understand that as much as the organization is interviewing you, you are - from your perspective - also interviewing them. Though the power dynamics are skewed towards the employer, this is your opportunity to pay attention to further signs that this organization fits you. At this point, I look out for the most subtle signs in tone, vocabulary, body language, energy, enthusiasm, lack thereof, and the questions they ask me. This is the time to look at the experience with social intelligence and emotional intelligence. If you spot arrogance or disinterest in you at a "human" level beyond your significance to the payroll, then it's worth taking a moment and reflecting on whether this is where you want to be.

During the interview process, mentally assess if the parties interviewing you, the job description and your understanding of the job description align. When offered the opportunity to ask questions, pick out key points and pose questions along those lines. The goal of posing such questions is to ensure that your manager and other parties interviewing you have a unified view of their expectations for their ideal candidate.

Just as you may lack some of the ideal qualities that an organization is looking for in the role that you're vying for, on the other hand, organizations that you're considering working for may also lack some of the desirable elements of your dream workplaces. In such cases, you need to reflect inward and ask yourself: what are "must-haves" and what can you do without? This is something that requires honesty within yourself.

There should be harmony between what you have to offer the organization, the compensation plan, and the opportunity that working in that organization offers. When I've been interviewed, I appreciate organizations that see both my expertise and personality as advantages for them, if they choose to hire me. When I notice that a potential employer may find my personality ill-fitting for their organization, I pay attention to that area of misalignment.

Creating Your Team

There are three main phases of creating a new team: understanding or deciding on the selection criteria for hiring, interviewing candidates, and making select candidates offers. Let's talk about understanding or deciding on the purpose and mission of your team.

Understand the Purpose and Mission

"Getting the right people on the bus" means you need to understand what seats need to be filled on your bus and what role they should fill. By this, I mean you have to have a firm understanding of your team's purpose and the mission assigned to you. Make sure you understand the organization's goals and objectives. If you don't, seek clarification through documentation or ask the right people. To accomplish this, you may need to study the organization chart. I like to look at it without the names of individuals. This helps me focus on the interactions, reporting structure, and hierarchy without being distracted by personalities and their underlying influence. After all this groundwork, you should be equipped with a firm understanding of everything you need to know.

Criteria for Hiring

In Chapter 1, we looked at several dynamics that impact the team you find yourself with. I highlighted the qualities that make a great leader and team. If you noticed, I didn't say much about technical skills. As you can imagine, the technical or professional skills that your team will need will vary for your specific use case. In cybersecurity, I often look to fill the following roles: architect, engineer, and operator. "Architect" is the role of people who design the work. "Engineer" is the role of the people who build the work, and "Operator" is the role of the people who work on what was built. Your use case may not need these types of roles. Figure out what your team and organization need. Understand and define those roles.

Apart from the character traits I look for in team members and the specific technical skills required of a given role, I also look for the following: hunger, passion, willingness to learn, teachability, verifiable references, and genuine interest. "Hunger" in this case, is what Apple's late co-founder Steve Jobs once encouraged fresh graduates to do: "Stay hungry, stay foolish...[29]". I want hungry team members because they will focus on growth and curiosity. They will not be satisfied with mediocrity. They will yearn and strive for the better, given the opportunity. Being hungry is also a huge advantage when your team functions in a fast-evolving industry. That innate drive is a significant advantage.

There are highly qualified people with admirable technical skills who lack the will to learn. Maybe they used to

---

[29] Strauss, Valerie . "Steve Jobs told students: 'Stay hungry. Stay foolish.'". The Washington Post. 2011, October 5.
https://www.washingtonpost.com/blogs/answer-sheet/post/steve-jobs-told-students-stay-hungry-stay-foolish/2011/10/05/gIQA1qVjOL_blog.html

have it and lost it down the line. Maybe they are unwilling to learn because they feel they've "arrived" and no one else can add to their existing body of knowledge. Whatever the case, this attitude does not help high-performing teams. The willingness to learn is rooted in a sense of humility. When we can humble ourselves and accept that there may be gaps in our knowledge, we open the gates to new knowledge and even more opportunities wherever we are and wherever we would like to go next. Being willing to learn includes teachability. There is an ease to collaborating with team members who are reasonably receptive to guidance and other types of feedback.

Having references can challenge new graduates with virtually no work experience. I understand how frustrating that scenario must be for those joining the work world. I have two daughters early in their careers, and they are facing such challenges, too. It helps them do some volunteer work or even unpaid internships to build up their resume to overcome this limitation, to some extent. With some roles, having a portfolio of your work, for example; code, designs, and sample written works, can give them an added advantage over candidates who do not submit such evidence of their expertise.

"Genuine interest" is such an appealing attitude to

discover in a candidate. There's nothing like seeing someone light up with enthusiasm as they talk about the work that they get to do. When that genuine interest includes a positive emotional connection to the work or subject, then we have passion. Passion is magnetic and a joy to witness in any context.

Imagine building a team with those soft skills I presented in chapter one, the technical skills they need to do the work, and these additional traits I mention: hunger, willingness to learn, teachability, possessing references, and genuine interest. Can you see why you would, all factors being equal, ultimately create your dream team? I believe this approach would help you select ideal teams consistently and for as long as you are a leader.

Preparing for the Interview

The Human Resources department at your organization may have a checklist or other type of document for you to fill during the interview. Whatever the case, ensure you have adequate documentation prepared for each interview. I go to each interview with a script, a checklist, and a notepad. The script includes all the important questions I need to ask each individual. It also ensures that I don't forget to ask any important questions. The checklist is for my process and also for the HR department. This ensures that I supply HR with the documentation they need to back up the hiring process, and the notepad is for my notes. In my documentation, I ensure I prepare to note down each candidate's strengths and weaknesses. In preparation for your interviews, deciding what qualities and skills are must-haves and which ones you can do without is in your best interest.

If you ask me how many must-haves you need to identify for you to make a decision, then I'll have to tell you that it depends. Every context is unique, and it's up to you to diligently determine how many skills are enough and have some data to back up your reasoning. I tend to make some of my decisions using my intuition, but I don't let my intuition be my deciding factor. Rather, it directs me, and the data (from the interview and their application package) confirms that I've arrived at the right outcome.

The Documentation

Once the interview is over, the quality of your documentation will determine if you make a thorough and fair assessment. This is why taking sufficient notes is important because you can not remember everything. It's important to refer back to the strengths and weaknesses that you found relevant for the role.

Typically, I prepare the usual warm-up questions and

deeper questions. The deeper questions are necessary because questions like, "Who are you?" and "What makes you excited?" are not enough. These deeper questions are specific to the job I'm hiring them for. Questions about their education, what skills they possess, and what software programs they are proficient in are beneficial for hiring individuals to fit technology-heavy roles. If you want them to lead one of your teams, you may ask them about their experience managing projects and how they overcame challenges in any past projects they led or were an active part of.

The Interview

Let me let you in on a little secret. When interviewing candidates for my team, I can typically tell within 10-15 minutes of the interview if the interviewee is going to fit well on the team. Now, previously, I would not admit this to many people but it's true. Those initial minutes of the interview tell me whether we are going to gel or not and whether this new person will get along with the rest of the people already on the bus. I believe this is because I've trained my intuition over the years to look out for certain aspects in individuals, and the verifiable skills certify my eventual decision.

Now, even though I decided extremely fast, it does

not mean I cut the interview short. I am thorough in my evaluation of whether the candidate fits my hiring criteria. Another reason I invest time in completing the interview with candidates I already know will not be on my team is because I understand how impactful a poor interview can be for any of us. I want to have constructive feedback for them if they ask me why they were not hired. Just like each one of them, if I am not hired for a role, I want to know why and what I could have done better or where I was deficient in the interview. I believe we can do a lot better in responding to candidates we don't hire who request our feedback. Canned responses are not helpful. Now, I know this has nothing to do with the team that you intend to build. However, it has everything to do with being a decent human being. This is because it is an easy kindness to another human being, just trying to make it like the rest of us. Your feedback could even be the catalyst for their evolution, making them the first-choice candidate elsewhere.

In the previous section where I discussed documentation, I talked about the kind of documentation you need to prepare. You should come out with more information during the interview to influence your decision. As I interview candidates, I like to note down something about the candidate that caught my attention and made an impact on my impression of them. This could be something they said. In some cases, it could be the glimmer in their eyes, an aspect of their body language, their passion, enthusiasm, and hunger. In other cases, it's something that they said. A candidate presenting textbook answers to me in response to my questions may not get my interest as another candidate saying, "You know, what excites me about this role is..."

The great thing is that even if you conduct these interviews virtually, you can still pick up on subtle body language and other non-verbal cues if you are observant. To a lesser degree, you can still pick up on some of these calls, even over audio-only calls, because of hesitations, tone of voice, vocabulary, and the emphasis that the individual places on something they respond to. "Energy" can not be faked, and you can pick up on the interviewee's energy or attitude and genuine enthusiasm regardless of the interview mode.

Selecting a Candidate

It's highly unlikely you'll consistently find candidates who check all your boxes, and that's fine. What is crucial, though, is to understand and have your must-haves or non-negotiable criteria. One criterion that I find unnecessary to focus on on many occasions is a four-year degree. Yes, there are some fields where this makes absolute sense to categorize as "a must-have". However, there are many fields, especially in emerging technology (like Artificial Intelligence, cybersecurity, robotics, and design), where the individual's demonstrable skills may speak for them far better. In fact, on some occasions, I dialogue with the HR department to adjust job descriptions. These adjustments were to make accommodations for qualified people who didn't meet their minimum requirement of a four-year degree but had every other quality we needed in that particular context.

Now, I know that typically, most people making the hiring decisions select the smartest and most qualified individual on the candidate list. After all, they have the expertise and skills in the domain you want to hire for. Yes, we ought to hire people based on the subject matter, expertise, skill level, and cultural fit. But here's the thing: sometimes, the smartest candidate on your list may make for a terrible choice for you. Here's an example: that seemingly outstanding candidate (on paper) may have the biggest chip on their shoulder. If that person presents themselves as a know-it-all, they will make it challenging for the rest of the team to work with them.

This is a huge piece that I think many leaders overlook: focusing on the superstar (on paper) and ignoring the talent that presents all the abilities to rise to the occasion if only given a fair chance.

If a candidate checks all the boxes but lacks proficiency in technical skills, I consider whether they are willing to learn and if they are teachable. If they are, they stand a much better chance of getting selected than someone with those technical skills but lacks the soft skills I desire my teams to embody.

Making the Offer

After you select your candidate from the interview pool, it's time to make them an offer. Making the offer involves three aspects: what the candidate wants, what the organization can pay, and how willing and able the organization is to bridge any difference. Even though the interview process is technically over, I find it an ideal point to determine the candidate's motives.

I like to find new hires that don't have their focus only on the money element. Oftentimes, if the focus is just on the money, the discussion may lead to negotiations. There is nothing wrong with negotiations, but when the focus is primarily there, an organization may lose a candidate who happens to be a great fit because of failure to agree on a higher compensation plan.

Of course, losing a candidate because an

organization is unwilling to pay over a given range is standard, especially in cybersecurity and the IT industry. However, it's worth keeping in mind that salary ranges can vary widely depending on the industry of the job and the size of the organization hiring. For example, non-profit organizations typically don't have as sizable offerings as Fortune 500 companies. In my role as Chief Information Security Officer (CISO), some organizations offer annual salaries of $100,000 to $ 200,000. Larger enterprises are willing to pay you up to $ 800,000 annually for the same role. So, in some cases, organizations excited about a candidate may not have the budget for what some candidates may desire.

I like to find candidates who are motivated by fair-to-great compensation plans and the opportunity for the candidate to grow in their expertise in a great team, doing meaningful work. When I sat in the interviewee chair, my focus was more on this too. I need to feel fulfilled and challenged in the work I contribute to the world.

Here's an example of a package that may not sound great when you look only at the salary but actually offers a lot to appreciate: An annual salary of $80,000 that includes 2 weeks of training every year, four weeks of paid vacation, and the opportunity to work in the office only two days a week. When a candidate looks at such an offer objectively, they may find it quite appealing, even in comparison with a higher paying job that requires your full presence at the office every week and occasionally on weekends, and no real training opportunities for the candidate's growth. Can you see the difference in value?

I've hired people to my team who were excellent candidates but, due to their circumstances, felt willing to accept considerably lower salaries. I've had other candidates who specialized in certain areas and found their desires more focused on the financial aspect, possibly because of the extensive investments they made in upgrading their academic and professional skills. They considered their investments towards mastery justifiable for higher salaries. Justifiable or not, if an organization doesn't have the resources, then an agreement will not happen between the two parties. However, if this second individual interviewed for an organization that had the budget for them, their chances of getting the job are higher.

I've also seen inexperienced graduates expecting large salaries. These salaries are what others in the industry spent years working toward. In these cases, these fresh graduates find themselves disappointed when organizations are simply unwilling to pay them what they express, even if those organizations have the budget. I wonder, in those cases, if their decision-making processes included considerations like growth opportunities, flexibility, location, and even the quality of the team that they would be joining.

So, other than a fair salary, flexibility, location, training opportunities, and networking opportunities, the purpose of the work can also be genuinely valuable. Each candidate knows what's most important for them, and everyone's choices are valid, even if we fail to agree during the offer phase.

Often, it's a good idea to offer candidates salaries that allow upward growth. If a negotiation leads to the top end of the range, and your company has strict protocols for salary bands, then when that employee does an excellent job for several years, they will eventually need a promotion or to find another job elsewhere. Having some upward wiggle room in terms of the salary secures the presence of that individual for the opportunity of salary increases when the time comes.

Optimizing pre-existing teams

Now that we've completed how to approach creating your teams, it's time to look at how you can optimize pre-existing teams. Let me begin with a quick story of my own.

I inherited a team at a new job I was grateful to find. The team wasn't functioning well when I arrived. Something wasn't right. When I did my gap analysis, I discovered several unfulfilled roles and responsibilities. My initial approach was to try and get members of the existing team to fit into some of these empty slots. Fortunately, when I met with one of my coaches, he helped me realize fairly quickly that my approach was flawed.

"Tammy, you're doing it backwards," said my coach.

And he was right. With his help, we formulated the approach that I share with you in this section. First, identify the roles and responsibilities required in the team. Then, understand the people you have - in terms of capabilities. Lastly, identify the gaps and decide how you would close those gaps by either hiring internally or externally. This said, let's look at the roles and responsibilities of your team first.

Roles and Responsibilities

Whatever role you need filling, in the ideal scenario, you want it filled by someone who has experience in that role. You would want someone conversant with the responsibilities and how to handle that role daily. In some cases, this may be a challenge. This is sometimes the case, oftentimes in highly specialized roles. However, you can address this challenge by assigning this role to someone willing to learn, is teachable, and is enthusiastic. You can either find someone from within your existing team or hire externally.

I don't know how you approach this scenario right now but let me share with you an experience I had myself several years ago in optimizing a pre-existing team.

"I've seen Tammy take a team of people that came to work each day, sat down at their desks, did their job, and left, day in and day out. So, when Tammy took over that team, I saw those people change. They started to come into work smiling, greeting their workmates, and pleasantly interacting with one another.

I believe that's because Tammy empowered them to make decisions in their jobs. Previously those people would come to work with great ideas on how to do things better, but nobody cared. So they just continue doing the same thing.

When Tammy came along she interacted with them and sought them out for their opinions and insights. She asked them questions and involved them. The whole dynamic of the group made a 360-degree turn. Everybody in her team was strikingly different."

- Mary-Sue

Understand The Team

When I say "understand the team", I mean you ought to understand each team member as a person. What makes them tick? What interests them? What are the areas of professional growth would they love to take on but haven't yet been empowered to?

Typically, people may caution you about getting this close to your team. The idea is that some people will not want to talk about their personal lives, which is a legitimate concern. However, this approach has always worked for me because I believe knowing about each team member and their lives is crucial. I care about them, and I think it's a natural by-product of that care. Each team member matters to me more than the role they fill in my team. They matter because they are human beings, just like me. My team knows that I'll ask about how they and their family are doing. If their kid had a baseball game, they know I'll ask how it went. If their spouse is ill, they find it normal for me to follow up and ask if they are feeling any better. For me, this is the most human approach to working with fellow humans. Any other way doesn't resonate with me.

Typically, this approach leads to us developing a rapport and connection with one another. When we have to discuss work and issues to do with their performance or any gaps I see in the team, they know I'm coming at them as someone on their side and not as some opponent.

Now, you may not be a proponent of this approach, but time and time again, I've received feedback from my team about the value this has offered to them. Here's one story a former reporter told me that touched my heart:

"... My dad passed while I was working with Tammy. I happened to be in another city so Tammy and I were talking over the phone. Tammy concluded the conversation with, "Give Mom a hug for me".

It really stuck with me. At the time, I needed a lot of emotional support myself, and that sentiment for my mother was so validating on behalf of my mom and my own experience. I will never forget that...."

- Wentworth

Just asking someone if they are okay, especially at a time like the CoronaVirus pandemic when their world was turned upside down, meant so much to many people. This included myself. In addition, some people found that home wasn't always a happy place. The CoronaVirus pandemic forced these people to be at home far longer than healthy, creating a toxic dynamic when they would have had their onsight work-world as a respite. So, when I had the opportunity to check in with my team, I took it. I was glad to assist them where I could provide a reasonable level of support due to their willingness to share.

I would also ask them if they would prefer to talk to someone else; in the event that talking to me about their concern felt too heavy of an exercise. In those cases, I was happy to arrange that for them.

All this taught me the importance of acknowledging everyone's lived experiences, even in the context of a work dynamic. Even if some people chose not to share what may have been upsetting them, I still felt making them aware that the door was open and they were welcome to come to me or someone else they might prefer was necessary. As you understand your team, you know not only who they are but also what they are dealing with. You also learn how to support them and, in some cases, which roles to place them in to maximize their strengths, help fulfill their desires, and grow their contribution to the team.

Identify the Gaps

If your team was dysfunctional to begin with, and you spent time understanding the roles and responsibilities and coming to understand your team, then you should be at a point where you recognized some gaps.

If you reach this point, you must choose between two options. Your first option is to allow existing team members who don't fit these roles the opportunity to fill a given but vacant role. Your second option is to look for a new hire externally to fill this vacant point.

In my case, I always make sure to offer members of my team the opportunity to take up the job if they feel that they can rise to the occasion. This is particularly in case the specific team member in question isn't meeting their job requirements as expected. Additionally, I always take this approach when dealing with team members that I inherited from a previous leadership and happened not to select myself.

When I come to this realization and offer an employee this choice, it's up to them to take up the offer or decide to find a job opportunity elsewhere in the organization or externally. If they decide to look elsewhere, you have to start rolling out offboarding procedures to make it a smooth transition for their departure. I share with you how to navigate that in the "Offboarding" section.

If an employee decides to take up the challenge, their evaluation period in this new role is typically 90 days. Now, this does not mean we have one conversation and I meet up with them 90 days later to inform them of the verdict. No.

During this period, it's an active conversation to ensure that they are adequately supported as they try to fill their new role.

In either case, my goal is to help that member of the team come to their own realizations about what is in their best interest and that of the team regarding their performance. Either option is an attempt at guiding them to control the situation instead of having to deal with a situation that they feel "happened to them".

If significant gaps remain after the 90-day assessment period, then it's time to go back to this employee and begin the discussion about offboarding. At the same time, it means actively looking for a capable team member to take up their role as we begin the hiring process to replace this individual who unsuccessfully went through the 90-day assessment period.

This is a very unpleasant part of the leadership process, I know. However, one pleasant thing about this process that I would like to share with you is that oftentimes, you don't have to fire underperforming team members. Oftentimes, they come to this realization themselves and take the initiative to resign. Many of us do not like being perceived as the bad guy, so this certainly takes out the sting in experiences of this nature.

Onboarding

If the candidate accepts the offer you presented, great! It's time to onboard them. Onboarding involves welcoming new team members into the fold, orientation, and embedding them into the team. This process may last anywhere up to 90 days. Typically, the first two weeks are the most intensive of this phase for new team members.

The Welcome

"The Welcome" can be neglected in some organizations, and I find it's crucial to create that first impression that we know will last a lifetime for those who become part of your team. Let me share with you a particular situation that convinced me firsthand of the importance of a warm welcome in any organization for new employees:

It happened 31 years ago. I was excited about my first job in technology and couldn't wait to prove myself in corporate America. The role was challenging, but I had a level of confidence that I felt could carry me through. Dressed to impress in my red dress, my naive twenty-year-old corporate self stepped into the giant establishment and reported to HR on my first day.

"Oh, we don't know where to put you yet," said the

HR as she shifted uncomfortably in her seat. I tried to contain my obvious disappointment and surprise.

Now, at the time, this organization had a career development program. This program meant that when you joined the organization in your early career phase, you received training across the board. This allowed them to determine where you would be best suited. At this point, they hadn't determined where that would be. Perhaps you can imagine the feeling of concern and unease that this presented me with.

When I was ushered to meet my new boss, though he exuded warmth, he, too, hadn't been expecting me.

"Here you go," he said as he handed me a stack of books.

No one's first day at work needs to be like this. Being received well anywhere sets the tone and initial level of engagement of new team members. It tells them that they made the right decision to join your team. Fortunately, I had a solid and pleasant experience in this company for many years. My bosses were typically marvelous individuals. I am glad this experience didn't put me off entirely. But sadly, it did teach me why offering your new employees the attention you would expect on day one is imperative.

A good welcome should include a reasonable amount of preparation. If they expect an office, make sure you have it ready, or at the very least, you have their temporary space ready for them to get settled in. If your office does team breakfast meetings, maybe you could use that as an opportunity to welcome them on board. You could instead walk the person around and give them quick one-to-one introductory experiences with the other members of the team. Whatever approach you take, make sure you highlight to them the individuals in the organization they should develop relationships with.

You also want to ensure they have all the tangible resources they need to do a great job. Do they have a phone, laptop, organizational email address, and whatever else they need to do a seamless job? If not, get it to them.

Orientation

After you've made these efforts to make your new team member feel welcome, it's important to sit down with them and review important information about their presence in the team, what your leadership offers, and your expectations from them. Their job requirements, team objectives, and goals for their work are some of the things you want to make sure you review. You especially want to ensure you review with them and present documented goals to them.

Some people take longer than others to get settled, and that's normal. To help my new team members with their orientation, I like to assign a "buddy" to them. This is a person whose unofficial job is to help orient them to their new environment and all the ins and outs. Essentially, it is someone who metaphorically "holds their hands" until they are on their feet. I recommend you consider this approach because you won't have time to do this yourself. The goal is for this new team member to feel directly supported for the first days or weeks until it's reasonably possible to let them navigate the workplace like the rest of the team. If they have any questions, I want them to feel comfortable coming to me or even this "buddy" I introduced them to.

Embed in the Team

Another aspect of the onboarding process is what I like to call "Embedding in the Team". I want every new member to feel firmly rooted in my team. I direct each new team member to meet with every team member individually and discuss what their role is and what they've learned in their job. I want the other team members to share with this new person what challenges they faced and what they wished they had known on day one when they each took up their roles. The goal of this exercise is to foster a sense of camaraderie and cohesion among all team members.

If this new team member needs to interface with other business partners, both external and internal, you may need them to spend some time talking to each key partner. The goal here is to ensure they understand what the organization does and who they do it with. If you have field sites, you may direct them to visit one site so that they get to understand what the business does. You want them to make the connection between what the business does and what their daily role contributes to the organization's success.

You need to ensure that each new member understands that the rest of the team is in the same boat as them. You also need to make clear to them which boat they happen to be in, which direction you are steering them to, where you intend to get to, and how we will all accomplish this together.

Offboarding

At some point, some of your team members may need to exit your team. As you know, circumstances will vary as to why. Circumstances include: If they consistently failed to meet the expectations set out in their job description, if they declined to take up a role identified through your gap analysis when their pre-existing role no longer fit the structure of the team, or if they were exceptional and found opportunities elsewhere in the organization or externally. Whatever the case, these scenarios require you to start the offboarding process.

I like to consider that there are three components to the offboarding process: the transition plan, timing, and the exit. Let's take a moment to talk about each of these.

Transition Plan

In a real-world scenario, the circumstances surrounding the employee's departure will greatly impact how thoroughly you implement a transition plan. The transition plan is heavily dependent on the initiator. In the case that your employee was removed because of inadequate performance, it may be challenging for all parties involved to carry out your plan because the outgoing employee may not feel adequately incentivized to cooperate. After all, if they disagree with the transition, they may find it very difficult to cooperate. In other cases, some people fired from their roles remain cooperative. Since we are all human beings who respond to things differently, it's important to accept that sometimes the outcomes can be unpredictable and even unpleasant.

I always aim to execute a thorough transition plan

because the team and organization may suffer without it. Without an effective plan, there can be gaps in information, disturbance to the workflow, and confusion among the remaining staff and stakeholders. It can also become a breeding ground for gossip and other undesirable behaviors that I find intolerable in any team I manage.

Let's look at some major components of a transition plan that you might want to incorporate:

➢ The transition plan must highlight key activities that the individual leaving was working on and to whom these activities will be transferred.

➢ There must also be a "knowledge transfer" session between the outgoing employee and the person taking up their responsibilities. In that session, all important information needs to be passed on. The best "knowledge transfer" sessions, in my opinion, are those conducted in person. This allows the person taking up the role to ask any questions they have in real-time, ensuring the smoothness and comprehensiveness of the knowledge transfer.

➢ In many cases, you may not have a new person ready to take up their specific role. In such scenarios, you have to identify someone within your team who is capable of holding down the fort until you are in a position to employ someone suitable. In other cases, this may not even be an option. In those scenarios, the wisest thing may be to shut that person's activities down until you can employ someone new to fit the role. This sometimes looks like temporarily shutting down a project, especially when that employee was integral in its functioning.

> ➤ An exit message from the outgoing employee: If the outgoing employee is willing, you may ask them to send an email to the rest of the team and other key stakeholders. The intention of this email is not only to say farewell but to ensure transparency and understanding as to what is underway.

> ➤ If the employee is unwilling to send out an exit message or neglected to do so, you should send out one on their behalf. Here is an example of what you, as a leader, could write on their behalf if they are leaving after an unsuccessful 90-day assessment in their new role offered to them after a gap analysis: *"... As a result of personal choices / changes in the organization, Carlton has decided to leave the organization to pursue alternative opportunities elsewhere. As a result of this transition, this is who you should be contacting in the event: ..."* This is a very important step because you do not want your key stakeholders in the dark and wondering who to turn to after the change.

➢ If you source a replacement internally (on either a temporary or permanent basis), you have to ensure that you introduce this new person to all key stakeholders, at the very least, over email. You want to ensure that everyone knows who will be handling their requests or any other activities that the outgoing employee formerly had the responsibility to handle. You will also have to adjust their pre-existing workload and remove some things off their plate to accommodate these extra responsibilities they will take on.

➢ Availability of documentation of everything important is also crucial. You have to make sure that documentation is secure and in a place where relevant staff can easily access it. If your system only provided access to certain data to this outgoing employee, you have to make sure that this outgoing employee's account and permissions become invalid at the end of the transition phase. You also have to make sure that anyone taking up their responsibilities has an account and access rights to access and manipulate the data they need to execute their responsibilities successfully.

Timing

The second major component of the offboarding phase is timing. Again, timing, like your transition plan, is dependent on the circumstances involving this offboarding instance. Your preparedness, if the employee had a planned exit, will significantly differ in terms of timing, from one that was unplanned. If it was unplanned and their contract is being terminated with or without cause, the timing will also be affected. And if the employee's contract was terminated without cause, there are a lot of other additional legal factors that will come into play, and likely affect any timeline you would have preferred. When you have a planned exit, you are in the comfortable position of planning based on their final date of employment as they serve their notice period.

The Exit

The last major component of the offboarding phase is the exit. This is essentially the reverse of the welcome. I strongly believe in consistency when engaging with people in the workplace and beyond. It's worth carefully considering how you would want these people to leave the organization. You need to keep in mind that just as much as a poor welcome can impact a new employee, a poor exit can do as much damage. We are all human, and keeping that in mind as someone moves on is the most decent thing to do. One aspect of the exit plan that I believe you need to pay attention to is a recognition plan for the outgoing employee.

As I've stated several times, the circumstances of this employee's exit will affect such matters, including a recognition plan. If the events around this individual's exit are hostile or criminal, you would not celebrate them as an outstanding employee loyal to the company for a decade.

In an ideal scenario, the recognition plan does not have to be expensive or elaborate. I believe the most important component of it is that it is thoughtful and tailored to the person who's moving on. Depending on what is ideal at the time, you may wish to have a team lunch to send them off. In other cases, you may take just a handful of people from the organization with those exiting out for a special meal instead of the whole team. Or you can just bring delicious donuts to the office for everyone to celebrate your team member who's leaving. You can get creative with how you want to do this.

If the exit is hostile, you may wish not to create additional discomfort in an already uncomfortable situation. In that case, if you do something, you may decide to downplay it somewhat.

In circumstances where the employee has been around for a long period, you can let your celebration of them and their contribution be more elaborate and perhaps costly. Here's a delightful example of a great employee who made a huge impact on the company but had to eventually leave.

"Bradly had been in the organization longer than I. I think it was 30 years long if I'm not mistaken. Everyone in the organization knew him. He was everyone's go-to guy when you wanted to know something about the organization. We thought of him as our own historian and knowledge bank. He was a pleasure to work with and quite frankly, when I heard he was leaving, I felt pretty sad about it. Bradly was something of an institution... or shall I say "icon". He kind of symbolized something for many of us. He had this heavily fragrant cologne that only he wore. When he walked through the office corridors, his scent let you know that he'd just passed through. He also was the most dapper man I had ever seen! He came to work looking like the cover model of GQ Magazine, every day! I truly admired him. Many of us did.

Anyway, one day, we all received his exit message in our company emails. At some point, I remember Tammy called up Bradly's wife and asked her what cologne he wore. On Bradly's send-off, a team dinner, she put together some gifts for him that he was happy with. Tammy had a t-shirt printed with the word "Historian" on the front. She also had pictures of Bradly printed on these little cards she gave each *of us that she sprayed Bradly's cologne on for us to remember him by.*

Everyone had the opportunity to sing Bradly's praises and Bradly too had a moment to share his thoughts. I remember thinking how awesome it was to know you are thought of so well by people you worked with for so many years." - Mariah.

Though we didn't do the same thing for every employee who left, we always made sure that we did something thoughtful. Whether it was an intern that was around only for two months, we did something. On one occasion, when I had a summer intern, and I learned that her peer working at my colleague's department hadn't planned anything, I set up a small lunch at a decent restaurant where my colleague, our two interns, and 4 other people sat and celebrated these young people that had taken the time work diligently for our organization. My colleague told me he would never have thought about it otherwise. I hope these two interns look back on our leadership and organization with warm memories and an understanding that they were valued as people, even though they were only with us for two months. I know their contribution mattered, and I am grateful for that effort. The purpose of all this effort is to leave a positive imprint in their memories, a legacy that they may think back on with fond memories.

My Message to You

The reality is this is hard work. Perhaps not physically, but mentally and emotionally. You have to be deliberate and people-focused. Many dynamics come into play when dealing with people through different circumstances that further complicate your efforts in terms of adding team members, maintaining your team, and inevitably having to let some go for whatever reasons.

When someone needs to leave the organization, and it is not their preferred choice, you must be sensitive to their emotions and way of thinking. After all, you are dealing with people's sense of security, financial income, and ways of life. In light of this, I believe every leader needs to care.

So yes, I know the approach I shared in this chapter may sound exhausting. Leading effectively can be exhausting. If you are simply managing, you likely have an easier go of it. I recommend you revisit Chapter One to note the difference between a leader and a manager if the differences are lost. But yes, effective leadership is exhausting in some ways. There's an upside, though: leading in this way is always rewarding! I have never regretted the thoughtfulness and kindnesses I've expanded in the 30+ years of leading in corporate settings.

If taking a caring stance does not come naturally to you, but you would like to become a more effective leader, I strongly encourage you to invest in the growth of both your emotional and social intelligence. A great book to explore on emotional intelligence is *"Emotional Intelligence: Why it Can Matter More Than IQ"* by Daniel Goleman[30]. Another book by the same author worth reading on the topic of social intelligence that does a great job of breaking down its components and making the whole concept accessible to you is *"Social Intelligence: The Revolutionary New Science of Human Relationships"*[31].

Investing in becoming more emotionally and socially intelligent has many rewards, and as you attempt to grow in those areas, I want you to keep in mind that the rewards far exceed the hard work. Though I can not promise that things will get easier, I can promise that it may come more naturally over time. However, difficult circumstances are inevitable, so your experiences will depend on a case-by-case basis.

---

[30] Goleman, D. Emotional Intelligence: Why It Can Matter More Than IQ. 1995. Bantam Books

[31] Goleman, D. Social Intelligence: The Revolutionary New Science of Human Relationships. 2006. Bantam Books.

A quote attributed to Bruce Lee comes to mind as I close this chapter: "Practice makes perfect. After a long time of practicing, our work will become natural, skillful, swift, and steady.[32]"

We are now at the end of our chapter. Here, we talked about getting the right people on the bus. We also concluded with exiting some people from the bus. In the next chapter, titled "Team Norms" we will focus on the key elements of engagement that can help you keep the right people on your bus. Let's go.

---

[32] MS. "17 Practice Makes Perfect Quotes To Become The Best". 2023, October 1. https://findmotivation.org/practice-makes-perfect-quotes/

Chapter 3

Developing Your Team

"The ratio of We's to I's is the best indicator of the development of a team." – Lewis B. Ergen[33]

In Chapter 2, we focused on getting the right people on your bus. After successfully assembling a group of capable people, you need to develop that group of people into the team that you envision. In this Chapter, we will focus on just that: Developing your team. We will begin by looking at the operating principles that you may wish your team to adopt. Then, we will talk about the stages of team

---

[33] For Healthcare Research and Quality Agency. "Teamstepps: Team Strategies and Tools to Enhance Performance and Patient Safety Instructor Guide Issue 6, Part 20 of AHRQ publication". 2006. Government Printing Office.

development and the different interaction levels required to maintain a successful team. So, let's start by looking at the fundamental elements every successful team needs to operate by.

Operating Principles

From my leadership experience over the decades, I've discovered six fundamental operating principles crucial to team development. These principles are transparency, togetherness, inclusion, presence, participation, and consistency. What I like to call "TTIPPC", pronounced *"Tipsy"*. Let's explore these operating principles together.

Principle #1: Transparency

As far as it is possible to share information with your team without breaking your confidentiality agreements or any agreed disclosure concerns, it's important to ensure your team is given all the information they need. Sometimes, this can be challenging because it may be uncomfortable for you and for them to have certain conversations. If lay-offs are looming and times are turbulent, you may not want to be the bearer of such depressing news, but it comes with the territory of being a leader. It is better to prepare them with the possibility than see them blindsided because they never had the chance to prepare.

Principle #2: Togetherness

As the saying goes, "No one can whistle a symphony. It takes a whole orchestra to play it.[34]" Togetherness (unity and harmony) is the operating principle that results from all the other operating principles successfully being utilized. We can agree that we can achieve only so much alone, but with a vibrant and effective team, we can change the world. Togetherness is what makes that change or impact possible.

Principle #3: Inclusion

Great teams are inclusive. There are no playing favorites. In that vein, it's a great idea to ensure you, as a leader, are equally accessible to all team members. You must also ensure that every team member has the access and opportunity to contribute in meetings and as a team member as anyone else has.

Principle #4: Presence

It is never enough to be present for interaction with your team. If you are in a meeting, whether one-to-one, in pairs, or groups, your presence in that meeting needs to be fully engaged. You have to ensure you are free from any distractions, such as your phone, during scheduled

---

[34] Team Bonding. "115 Great Team Building Quotes". 2021. https://teambonding.com.au/100-great-team-building-quotes-part-1/

interactions with your team. Being fully present conveys to your team (and any other people) that you place great value in their presence and do not take them for granted.

Principle #5: Participation

Interactions need to be balanced, whether it's a one-to-one meeting or a meeting with two or more team members. It can't be a 30-minute or 1-hour-long session of you "talking at" the other party. It needs to be a back-and-forth, with a level of mutual engagement and involvement. Of course, team meetings are more structured, with team members contributing during the meeting at points set out specifically for their updates or feedback that's been expected from them.

Principle #6: Consistency

There are certain activities and responsibilities of team development that you and your team will need to do at varying levels of engagement or frequency. Some activities may need to be daily, others weekly, monthly, and even annually. When we look at Interaction Levels, we'll look at the specifics of this consistency. The bottom line is that the team development process is reliable, deliberate, and highly communicated to all relevant parties at the degree of disclosure they need to execute their jobs effectively.

Stages of Team Development

Regardless of your efforts at instilling operating principles, your team will grow through stages. According to Tuckman's model, you should anticipate at least five stages in your team's development[35]. These stages are forming, storming, norming, performing, and adjourning.

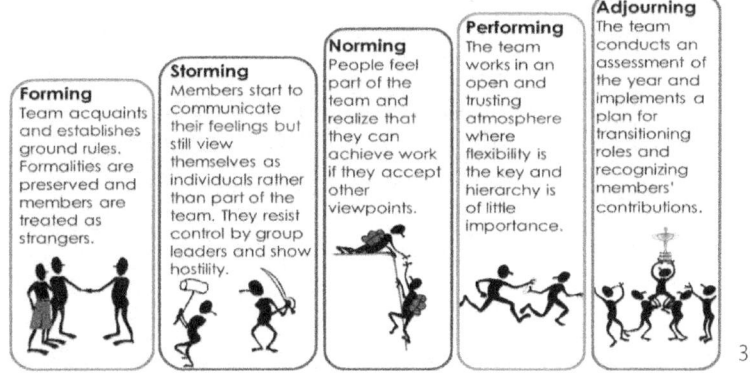

[36]

Source: https://i.pinimg.com/originals/f1/60/2b/f1602bce52996a9eddc7ab897ae2af02.png

I prefer to refer to the last stage as "continuous improvement" instead of "adjourning" because, ideally, you

---

[35] Stein, Judith. "Using the Stages of Team Development". Working on Teams. https://hr.mit.edu/learning-topics/teams/articles/stages-development

[36] Tuckman's Model. Pinimg.com. (n.d.). https://i.pinimg.com/originals/f1/60/2b/f1602bce52996a9eddc7ab897ae2af02.png

would aim for longevity when you have an effective team. I like to think that the Stages of Team Development from Tuckman's Model run in parallel to The Change Curve or Kubler-Ross Change Curve model that tackles how people deal with change[37].

THE CHANGE CURVE

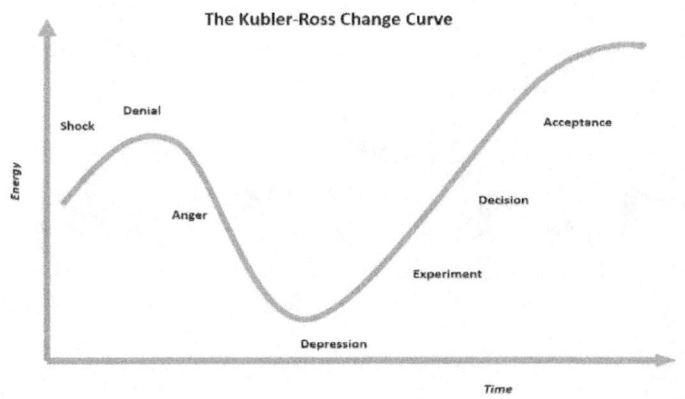

38

Source: https://changemanagementinsight.com/kubler-ross-change-

---

[37] Belbin. "Coaching people through the Change Curve with Belbin". The Change Curve. (n.d.). https://www.belbin.com/resources/articles-directory/the-change-curve

[38] Tahir, Umar. "Kubler Ross Change Curve Model". Change Management Insight. 2019, December 10. https://changemanagementinsight.com/kubler-ross-change-curve-model/

curve-model

Forming

The forming stage of your team's development is everything we discussed in "Chapter 2 - Getting the Right People on Your Bus". There, we looked at the onboarding process, choosing where you can lead, creating your team, optimizing your team, and offboarding team members. Feel free to flip back for a quick recap.

However, I will add one important matter. You need to ensure that you introduce yourself to all the relevant parties in your team, organization, and any external parties. I like to do this through a PowerPoint presentation titled "Who Am I?". Here's what one former direct report had to say about this approach:

"... I certainly had leaders that I've seen in the past come in with maybe a post-it and a couple of notes. Not Tammy. She had a PowerPoint presentation for her introduction.

Tammy's approach immediately showed me that this is somebody committed, someone taking things seriously. There she was, introducing herself to the team and showing us that she was a human being and had a life outside of work.

Essentially, she was stating "This was who I am, this is how I operate, and these are my expectations to begin with.

So, to me that was pretty cool... and a great starting point to our working relationship with her..." - Treyvon

For the rest of this chapter, we will draw your attention to the subsequent stages of team development. Those stages are storming, norming, performing, and continuous development.

Storming

As the name of the stage suggests, there is some considerable turbulence in this stage of group development. Before you can get into a state of reliable calm, some turmoil and even chaos are not only to be expected but normal in building any team, even the most successful. Developing a new team or optimizing one requires change. Change - regardless of what caused it - is what creates those waves. The magnitude of the change often directly relates to the magnitude of the waves.

As a leader, you may sometimes cause the "Tsunami" or "earthquake" that your team experiences. This could be because you started a new team altogether or chose to let some team members go. In other cases, it could be unprecedented events like the COVID-19 pandemic, the development of new sweeping policies and groundbreaking technologies. When it comes to the storming stage of team development, the change we normally see at this point is purely because of the normal growing pains of teams.

If you find your team is in this phase, it's important to realize that your team is undergoing a very uncomfortable experience. They experienced one way of doing things that they may have found worked well for them, and then they found themselves in the turmoil of this stage. To successfully transition from the storming stage to the norming stage, you will need to encourage an atmosphere of open dialogue.

Your people are feeling their way through what this new change looks like. If you are new to the organization, they are still trying to understand what you want from them. They want to know how they fit into your vision for the team. They also want to know if they fit in or if they will find themselves suddenly out of a job. The thought that they could potentially find themselves looking for a new job soon is stressful and a genuine cause of concern in some cases. There are a lot of questions, many of which may go unasked if you do not encourage your team to open up to you. One of the best things you can do in this stage is help each individual navigate through it by fostering those operating principles, especially transparency, inclusion, participation, and unity.

Do not be surprised to find that some of your team feel a sense of shock, anger, and maybe even depression during this period. You may even experience some hostility and resistance in this phase. This is expected as your team goes through the motions of the Kubler-Ross Change Curve. Some will experience a sense of great loss, and the impact of this change will reflect how deeply they are emotionally and mentally affected by the change. Keep the differences in how people respond to change in mind, as you lead your team.

Norming

If your team successfully moves past the strong and uncomfortable emotions in forming and storming, such as apprehension, shock, anger, and depression, and the overarching sense is that of acceptance, then your team has moved on to the norming stage of team development.

In this stage, "team norms" are firmly set. "team norms" are how your team will effectively work together for success. In this stage, team members not only know how they fit into a new or optimized team but are also beginning to function successfully in their roles. The processes may not run smoothly at this point, but you can see that everyone and the roles they play have started to align and gel.

Performing

As you notice less noise and more focus from within your team, you will find yourself transitioning through to the performing stage of team development. In addition to a sense of acceptance of the change from within your team, you will also notice a heightened problem-solving ability in your team. The acceptance and demonstrative excellence in problem-solving starts to reflect to your team, organization, and external parties as effectiveness and, ultimately, success.

The interesting thing that you may find is your team may identify themselves when they reach this phase. However, for that to happen, there will need to be cognizant of all the development stages and also be self-reflective. It reminds me of one interaction with a former team member years ago about just that:

"I was complimenting my team on what a great job they were all doing. At the time, I was getting great feedback from internal and external stakeholders about their performance. Then a member of my team asked, "Do you think we've reached the performing stage now?" His realization was a pleasant surprise for me because he was right: we had reached the performance stage of our team's development. That internal recognition and acceptance that

comes with going through that evolution was a delight to witness."

Sometimes, going through the team development process and developing operating principles that enrich your team, may have consequences that are further reaching than you could ever expect. Here's one story that I believe illustrates this quite well:

"We weren't quite sure what to expect of Tammy when she joined the organization and began heading our team. Before she joined, our team - IT Team - didn't have a great relationship with the Operations Team. In honesty, most of us didn't have a full understanding of what they did, and engaging with them was often an inconvenience.

So, when she joined she built trust and brought the team together. Somehow she established camaraderie among us as a team. I think that was super important. That's something that I had not seen from prior leaders.

What's interesting, I think is that though she started this in the team, it didn't stop there. Her efforts at building trust in the team extended to our colleagues in OT and other stakeholders. It seemed like that circle kept expanding and expanding and expanding. Ultimately, we ended up having a very smooth working relationship with OT and other stakeholders that previously we felt a lot of resistance and ignorance working with. She managed to break down those silos and helped us establish relationships that made everyone's work much more efficient and pleasant!"

- Chester

The unfortunate reality is that not all teams will reach the performing stage. Several factors that are outside of your zone of control can prevent you from reaching this phase. You need to know this to avoid putting unreasonable expectations on yourself and your team, if that is or becomes the case for you at some point. Some of the factors that you might encounter that may lead to an inability for your team to fully actualize its potential include an unfavorable company culture, unprecedented events, and the business/market forces I presented to you in Chapter One.

What's more, if you have to field change after change without the opportunity for the dust to settle, you can not establish a sense of stability for yourself as a leader or your team. In those instances, the best you can do is to establish team norms and a reasonable level of functioning.

Continuous Improvement (Adjourning)

As I stated at the beginning of this section, whilst

Tuckman's Model refers to this phase as "Adjourning", what resonates more with me is considering it as the "Continuous Improvement" phase. Again, that is because I believe we all want to ensure the longevity of high-performing teams for as long as possible. For you to accomplish that, you need to continuously measure yourself and your team against your accomplishments over the past years. You need to assess whether you've reached your desired goals, discuss where you haven't, and implement plans to ensure you meet any new or upcoming goals. Some of the questions you need to ask your team include "What do you think we need to do differently next year?", "What worked?", and "What didn't work?". The operating principles you set up will guide you on the frequency. Regardless of what you settle for, ensure any sessions for reviewing team performance are iterative and bidirectional conversations.

Arriving at this stage does not mean your job is done. No, team development is more cyclic than linear. You need to expect and plan for a continuous, deliberate, and consistent approach. Great leaders always look for ways to develop and improve their teams to drive them to continuous high performance. That said, we can agree that this is hard work.

As a leader, your primary job is to focus on the team.

Of course, you must be expertly versed in your expertise. In my case that's cybersecurity. For you, that might be entirely different. However, on top of your technical or professional areas of expertise, you also have to ensure that at least 50% of your leadership efforts are human-centered. And this hard work will be rewarding and satisfying at times. Other times, it may be painful and frustrating. However, all of the time, that's the job you signed up for. This is to be expected when dealing with people, their feelings, and their livelihoods and attempting to influence them within the framework of their team dynamics.

This process also demands you approach your team and yourself with a level of grace. When people feel threatened, they may express negative emotions, including hostile behavior. You must ensure that you stay true to yourself throughout the team development process, assert your boundaries, hold on through the rough patches, and take time to recalibrate and reset when you need a break.

Interaction Levels

Developing your team requires maintaining interaction with your team at various levels. In this section, we'll talk about the following five levels of interaction: Group, One to One, Accountability Partners, Decompression Sessions, and Managing Up.

Group Level

The first level of interaction we need to talk about is the group level. From my experience, ensuring you have at least one monthly meeting scheduled for your whole team is crucial to ensuring that you embody those operating principles I shared with you at the beginning of this chapter. Ideally, this meeting should always happen, even if it means shifting the date in the event of unavoidable rising engagement that you can not get out of. You have to ensure that you are always present for these meetings. Even if I had to travel, I would ensure I was virtually present for the meeting. You see, your consistent presence conveys to the rest of the team the value that you place on engaging with them and ensuring everyone is on the same page and everything is on track.

Where possible, I would share any updates that I had the right to share with my team. When that was not possible, I would make it clear to the team that I would let them know of any developments as soon as possible.

This meeting would always be accompanied by a presentation that would include important topical information, key dates of upcoming events, a snapshot of key performance indicators (KPI), updates, reminders of top priorities, the team norms expected at that time, and elements to encourage mutual understanding, inclusion, participation, transparency, and unity. Typically, this PowerPoint presentation would be under 20 slides long, with various members of the team taking time to present any updates about their responsibilities.

Let's take a closer look at some of these elements: top priorities, team norms, key events, and motivational moments.

Top Priorities

As you can imagine, a meeting of this nature covers a great deal. For efficiency's sake, we would identify top priorities for each sub-team to present. This would often appear as a single slide in the presentation. Each sub-team would then ensure an informed representative of their subteam was present for this group meeting to speak on behalf of their subteam in an informed manner about the projects they were responsible for. The understanding was that any representative of a sub-team would have enough know-how to make decisions during this meeting on behalf of their sub-team.

As a leader, you are aware of the top-level interests of the organization, and you have to ensure your team contributes to the successful realization at employee-level. Your job is to ensure your team understands how their efforts relate to and fit into that larger vision. Your team needs to come to an understanding of their efforts at a corporate level and not just operational or team level. Once there is that understanding, everyone can more easily conceptualize how their piece fits into the bigger picture of the puzzle. This gives everyone a voice and provides clarity. Including important topical information for relevant parties with key responsibilities further smoothens the process because everyone knows where to get something specific answered or done.

Team Norms

As with Top Priorities, Team Norms would appear as a single slide in the monthly presentation. In that part of the presentation, the team would be reminded what technology platform to resort to for team chats, where team documentation is stored, which team calendar to utilize, and reminders for other monthly events. Other monthly event notices included generic reminders of their one-to-one meetings with me, their meetings with partners, decompression session dates, and reminders of important behaviors. Reminders of behaviors that need to be internalized included *"learn to escalate before it gets escalated"* and *"learn to say no the right way"*.

Key Events

This is a part of interacting with your team at a group level that you must ensure you pay great attention to. If your team is diverse and from all over the world, the likelihood is that some of your team members will have different cultural and religious beliefs that you need to acknowledge as much as you would your own or those of the majority. There is a genuine need for sensitivity to ensure inclusion, equality, and respect for diversity.

In my case, I would often include a slide of upcoming holidays across the board, paying attention to ensure all team members' religious or cultural beliefs were remembered. Global teams meant that at the end of the year, we included Christmas, Boxing Day, Hanukkah, Kwanzaa, Omisoka, Bodhi Day, and other holidays as key events, including their respective dates. This ensured that we acknowledged and recognized the holidays of our colleagues in the team and understood when they may be out of the office and unavailable to attend to work demands for those dates. I would ask team members or they would sometimes volunteer to make brief diversity, equality, and inclusion presentations during this team meeting to share the significance of their cultural or religious beliefs, creating a wonderful learning experience for us all. It also allowed us to further live our team's operating principles, especially participation, inclusion, and unity.

Motivational Moments

Among the numerous qualities I listed in Chapter One as integral qualities of a great leader, being an inspiration was one of them. In fast-paced organizations with high stakes, stress tends to be high, too. To come to work and do a great job, day in and day out, without losing enthusiasm can be quite a feat at times. A great leader ensures they send some motivation your way any chance they get. I found that including one slide at the end of the team meetings was perfect for this purpose as we closed our meetings.

I would always ensure that the "motivational moment", as I called it, was relevant to whatever we were going through at the time as a team or as an organization. If we were experiencing excessive turbulence, I would put something in acknowledging that and attempt to offer some comfort through it. If times were more relaxed but people felt like they were treading water, I would find another creative approach to perking up their spirits. I felt it was important, with the motivational moment, to also ensure as a leader that I was not "tone-deaf" and unaffected by whatever the prevailing emotional and mental climate was in my team or organization. However, I always wanted my team to know that we could rise above it and strive to do our level best throughout.

Here are examples of motivational moments I would add to my presentations:

"All You need is faith, trust and a little Pixie dust" - *Peter Pan*[39]

To reinforce the above motivational moment, I decided to give each member of my team the little gift below.

---

[39] Barrie, J. M. *"All you need is Faith, Trust and a little Pixie Dust"*

— *J.M. Barrie, Peter Pan*" . Quotable Quotes. Quotes. GoodReads.com. https://www.goodreads.com/quotes/7440469-all-you-need-is-faith-trust-and-a-little-pixie

Source: https://www.etsy.com/listing/882771845/faith-trust-and-pixie-dust-key-chain?ref=yr_purchases

Here's another I found fitting as we approached the holiday season:

"This Christmas (holiday season) mend a quarrel. Seek out a forgotten friend. Dismiss suspicion and replace it with trust. Write a letter. Give a soft answer. Encourage youth. Manifest your loyalty in word and deed. Keep a promise. Forgo a grudge. Forgive an enemy. Apologize. Try to understand. Examine your demands on others. Think first of someone else. Be kind. Be gentle. Laugh a little more. Express your gratitude. Welcome a stranger. Gladden the heart of a child. Take pleasure in the beauty and wonder of the earth. Speak your love, and then speak it again."

- Howard W. Hunter[40]

One to One

Another level of interaction that needs to happen regularly for optimal team development is one-to-one interactions with your team members. These can take the structure of one-to-one meetings, typically lasting 30

---

[40] Hunter, Howard W. "This Christmas…". Quotable Quotes. Quotes. GoodReads.com. (n.d.). https://www.goodreads.com/quotes/688856-this-christmas-mend-a-quarrel-seek-out-a-forgotten-friend

minutes to an hour, once a month. In my case, I would schedule my one-to-one meetings with my team for the first week of each month.

During these meetings, you have to ensure that you are focused on the other participant and free from distractions. These meetings are more individualized or personal than groups or those you may have with partners. I would usually start these meetings with a personal catch-up. "How are you?", "How did Tommy do at his baseball game?", "Is your spouse feeling better?" are examples of some of the questions I opened with.

I like to take notes in a note-taking application like Evernote or OneNote for these meetings. However, I make it clear to everyone that I meet in one-to-one sessions that I am taking notes to be more effective in follow-up meetings. I made sure to state this so they did not assume I was attempting to multitask. It is important that your team members also know that you are not multitasking. Rather, you are taking them and their concerns very seriously and that they have your undivided attention. If you can not guarantee your undivided attention, the best thing that you can do in advance is offer them a different time slot when you know you will be far more likely to operate in a more collected manner.

As a leader, it is key for you to practice presence - one of the operating principles I highlighted at the start of this chapter. This level of interaction also requires active listening and documentation. These two aspects help you ensure that the other party is heard and appropriate responses are taken for any concerns they raise. Documentation also helps you overcome your limitations as a human being: forgetfulness. When you are busy with 101 things to do each day, it's easy for something you intend to accomplish to fall through the cracks. Taking great notes and following up on discussions helps you overcome that limitation.

If you want the best out of each of your team members, you have to be willing to ask the tough questions. That's why in my one-to-one sessions, I make sure I ask each team member questions like:

- Is there anything that I'm doing that is frustrating you?
- Is there anything that I should be doing differently?
- Is there something I should be doing for you that I am not?

When you pose such questions, you must ensure that you present them in a non-confrontational manner and that it must be bi-directional. It's not just you *"talking at"* them.

It's you two having a back-and-forth where you both know that you are on the same team with the same interests: to find a better way to get things done, with that "better way" being at the other end of this conversation as they answer these types of expository questions.

This approach also allows you to model and subtly guide your team on the type of interactions you would like them to emulate with other team members. In addition, this approach also helps you relate with your team members by validating their perspectives, emotions, and views as a primary focus. You accomplish this by being consistent in your acknowledgment of them and repeatedly letting them know that you've heard them.

Consistency and compassion is never a lost effort. Over time, it accrues, and your team knows that they can count on you to be the same person every day in terms of how you show up for them and how you help them to be successful in their roles. This rapport that you establish with them is worth its weight in gold. What's more, you can depend on it to count through the different experiences that may come your team's way.

Though the group meetings are quite structured, one-to-one sessions are not. One-to-one meetings call for an open dialogue approach. If your team member has something on their mind, this is the time to talk about it. Is there something they feel they've lacked from an experience perspective? Would they like to attend a particular training program to hone their skills? This is their time. Encourage them to use it wisely.

As the length of these meetings may vary, I always reserve the allotted time for that meeting. After some time of conducting these meetings, you may find that a meeting with one or two team members each takes far less time than that of others. In other cases, you may find some one-to-one meetings incredibly tedious and seemingly painful for you and the team member. I've noted this in the case of painfully introspective team members who prefer to hold their cards close to their chests. Decreasing the time allotted to them is tempting since you might have a considerable amount of time left over. It's also tempting to cancel these types of meetings entirely, to ensure you don't have to have this unpleasant experience.

However, I encourage you not to take such measures. Ensuring everyone has the same amount of time with you, regardless of whether they choose to utilize it or not, is about equality, inclusion, participation, and team harmony. Of course, sometimes, you might have to cancel a meeting or two because of emergencies and other pressing matters, but it should not be your go-to when you can make other accommodations elsewhere.

Admittedly, one of the biggest criticisms of this level of interaction with your team every month is how demanding it is regarding time and your effort as a leader. It is an incredible time commitment. This approach is ideal for smaller teams and becomes unsustainable the larger they are. So, if you happen to have 100 people reporting to you, you would need to adjust this approach to suit your needs. The first thing you would do is understand your span of control. How many people can you comfortably and realistically interact with monthly at this level? Then, you need to select direct reporters from this large number and delegate to them the responsibility of nurturing a certain percentage of your larger team. These need to be people who have caught your vision and can relate to others as you modeled for them. Keep in mind, though, that they can only model what you've successfully shown them. You need to ensure you've set the right tone and identified the right people to help you extend your reach and impact within your team at a one-to-one level.

One interesting observation I've noted over the years is that in one-to-one meetings, people often feel more comfortable asking questions about rumors and other concerns that they did not feel comfortable enough to present in a group setting. I don't believe there is such a thing as a bad question, so I try to respond as honestly as possible.

In cases where answering their question would lead to a breach of confidentiality, I also let them know that I am not in a position to answer those questions, but if things change, I'll get back to them with their answers. I also believe in telling my team I don't know when I genuinely don't have the answers they seek. It can be tempting, as a leader, to respond in ways that create the narrative of always having answers when you don't. This does not help in the long run because the truth sometimes rears its head and contradicts whatever false narrative you created. I suggest being honest about not knowing and offering to find out if that is at all a possibility. Maintain your integrity.

These one-to-one meetings are also excellent opportunities for your team members to share concerns about the performance of another team member who may not be pulling their weight. Let them air their grievances and ensure they offer concrete examples so that you have data to work with to address and help the team member in question if necessary.

Lastly, I encourage you to also use the one-to-one

encounters as opportunities to reaffirm your team members about their relevance and importance as part of the team. This is a golden opportunity to reassert the unity and harmony that makes your team chug along like a well-oiled machine.

Accountability Partners

To ensure seamless operations, I would pair up team members to help each other accomplish their jobs. If one was out of the office, sick, or otherwise unavailable, their partner would be responsible for ensuring that operations run smoothly. If I had group meetings scheduled and a team member was not able to attend, their accountability partner was mandated to make decisions on behalf of their accountability partners so that the meeting did not stall because of someone's absence. This, of course, required that both knew what the other was capable of and could make informed and genuinely actionable decisions in that regard. This would encompass all types of tasks, from the mundane to the mission-critical tasks.

In many cases, these partners would be individuals of significant opposite traits. I would pair a seasoned technician with a fresh graduate, an extroverted social butterfly with a very private introvert. The goal was to allow their opposites to balance them out. I ensured that roles and responsibilities were clearly defined when these partnerships were established. They had to invest significant amounts of time to ensure that they could successfully represent each other when circumstances demanded it. Essentially, these partners shared accountability and also ultimately enjoyed joint success. Naturally, I had to spend time strengthening their relationship for these two people to work well together. This often meant the two would have to engage each other every workday. These daily conversations and the strategies that they would agree to execute would help them establish a winning divide-and-conquer approach. This approach also helped them to remain aligned throughout the day, week, and month. As an aid to this setup, I met with each set of accountability partners once a month. As I would meet individual team members on the first week of each month, I scheduled accountability partner meetings on the second week of each month.

Oddly, meetings with each set of accountability partners felt much like couple's counseling, with me - the leader - being the counselor. As with any working relationship, challenges arise. When one person is saddled with far more work than their counterparts, these accountability partner meetings can help us get to the root of the problem and bring back balance and harmony.

Creating a successful dynamic of this nature requires deliberate work and effort. So, meeting with them helped me guide them toward the desired level of interaction.

Some of the questions that I would pose included the following:

- ➤ How is everything going between the two of you? Are you working well together?
- ➤ Where are you struggling?
- ➤ How can I help you both be successful?

After the introductory questions, I would switch gears and get more granular about their work. Here are some of the questions you may wish to ask your accountability partners in a meeting:

- ➤ What's going on in your area?
- ➤ How are you handling or managing the different activities you're being asked to participate in?
- ➤ How are you ensuring that you both are staying in sync?

In this setup, each member of the pair must participate, just as in a couple's counseling session. It's not of much use for anyone when just one person spends their time sharing their grievances in great detail while the other person sits in uncomfortable silence. It must be balanced and inclusive. For that reason, the leader must create a sense of safety for both members so that they feel comfortable enough to share their grievances, if any. Openness is encouraged so no one holds something back that could help make their sub-team and the team at large better than it is. If one of the pair is upset with the other, this is the time to get that conversation out to reach a reasonable and constructive conclusion on the matter. High-performing teams can not afford to sweep issues under the rug because such cosmetic short-term approaches only lead to growing resentment and bigger relational problems in the long term.

One happy aspect of the accountability partner setup is that it was often facilitated as a type of informal mentorship and coaching opportunity. This would work out well in many cases because it lacked the higher-pressure essence of a more formal arrangement but still had great benefits, especially in cases where a more junior team member was paired with someone more senior.

This accountability partnership or buddy system also offered additional benefits. Over a long enough time, you can start to see that they also managed to help sharpen each other's skills. Of course, the more junior or inexperienced team members would reap the most benefits with them reaching a level of expertise often at par with their more seasoned colleagues.

To ensure this approach worked without bias or unnecessary strain, I did something quite unconventional: I got rid of job titles within my team. Yes, they existed because the personnel department needed them for organizational purposes. However, I ensured everyone in my team knew that titles did not mean anything. This was to ensure equality among my team members. I wanted a junior team member to be acknowledged and respected as much as someone with extensive work experience. This is because the team is far more important than any titles, which were often arbitrary anyway. Instead of calling someone "Manager of Networking", I would call them "The Network Team", representative of the sub-team/ accountability partnership, roles, and responsibilities that they executed. When I took this approach, I found that much of the noise and contention arising from perceptions stemming from job titles faded away. It created a level playing field and helped flatten the "organization" of my team. The team was free to simply do their jobs without the unnecessary distraction of some words.

What I often find strange about titles is how you might have a role with the word "Manager" in the title, yet there is no role reporting to that title. Then, in that case, who are the managers? In case you are wondering, I, too, avoided using my title for the same reason. In one of my last positions, my title happened to be "Director of Information Security". I found this would often impede my desire to interact with my team on an equal footing because of the pomp that this title conveyed and the underlying understanding of how much I get paid. That pay grade, as it influences how people treat you, I opted to downplay my official title - as with those of my team. Instead, I used the title "Cybersecurity Leader" on my business cards.

In many instances, I've seen team members with junior titles working harder than other members with senior titles. These instances proved to me how unnecessary such titles were. Not being too fussed about titles also means you don't inadvertently create the impression that you have favorites when it comes to your team. I enjoy the equality that my "titleless" approach affords me and my team.

There are numerous benefits of the accountability partnership structure but let me be clear: many of the benefits I've shared in this section can only be enjoyed after the partnership has reached certain maturity levels. It is not something that typically works perfectly straight out of the door. It requires lots of deliberate effort and teamwork to nurture and sustain.

Decompression Sessions

In fast-paced environments, it is easy for the atmosphere to be a frenzied "Go-go" work experience with no hope of catching your breath. For that reason, I built into my team development experience what I called "Decompression Sessions". A decompression session is a time (often one and a half hours long), during office time, when my team and I de-stress or decompress. As with the group team meetings, one-to-one, and accountability partner meetings, decompression sessions also occurred once a month, but on the fourth week of the month.

What I would do during a decompression session would vary. Sometimes we would go to the snack bar across the street as a team, enjoy a few drinks, and relax. On other occasions, I would plan an actual activity like ax throwing. On numerous occasions, we would all go out of the office for breakfast together. Most of the time, when I scheduled these activities, I made sure to cover the costs from my resources and not that of the team or the organization. At times, I would not have any activity planned for our decompression sessions. In those cases, I might instruct the team that though the decompression session was not canceled, there was no event set up, and instead, they could use those 1.5

hours to write their performance review or another activity they found relevant.

Of course, carrying out joint activities when your team is distributed around the globe can be quite tricky. Geographic differences and, of course, time zone differences are significant factors. To overcome geographic limitations, I would delegate the coordination of these sessions to a responsible team member where team members were located further away. For example, if I scheduled bowling for our Decompression session for our US-based team, I would encourage our team in India and elsewhere to also have an event of their choosing for their enjoyment at a time that was reasonable in their timezone.

Can you see why sessions like these might be an excellent addition to your team's calendar? Apart from these sessions keeping your team's work-life interesting and fun, they also helped factor in the needs of most human beings for community, comradery, and relaxation. At one company where I had decompression sessions - then called "Chill Time", we would go across the street to have chips, salsa, and beverages at 3:30 p.m. This allowed the team to let out any frustrations, laugh, and sometimes even cry.

One of my former leaders inspired these sessions through voluntary monthly happy hours. For many of us who worked there for many years, even after these happy hours eventually ceased, we continue to meet once a month. Continuing this tradition was an initiative I took because of the value of our relationships. We still get together long after the company was purchased, and many of us moved on to different opportunities. Through these informal interactions, some of our deepest and most enduring friendships were inadvertently formed.

As simple a concept as Decompression sessions sound, the exercise of consistency, presence, relaxed participation, and inclusion helps build the unity and harmony that all teams have. There's something regenerative about stepping out of the office for a moment with colleagues and allowing yourself to just breathe. Of course, during these relaxed moments over chips and salsa or as we bowled, I took them as opportunities to update the team on other company events and discussions they needed to be aware of.

Engaging with my team at the human level is vital. That's why I often go above and beyond when I have the means to. Here's an example that was not exclusive to a decompression session but still illustrates the spirit of togetherness, care, and harmony that I strive for:

"...Tammy invited us to her house for Thanksgiving

day and she was incredibly hospitable. She prepared everything and cooked dinner for us.

She always displayed certain gestures that helped us feel cared for and valued. Sometimes she wouldn't just send Christmas cards, she would send chocolates and treats for us in the mail.

I had bosses in the past who would sign a Christmas card and give it to you but never this level of care. I remember our team here in Asia receiving chocolate and cookies from her.

And you know what? Even after she left the organization, we stayed in touch. When I would visit the United States, I'd make sure to ask her for lunch or dinner so that we could catch up.

To this day, I've never had a boss like her...."

- Kim

Managing Up

The last level of interaction you need to ensure you have regularly is with the leaders you report to. First, you must ensure that all leaders know who you are and what role you play in the organization. Hopefully, you will get this opportunity when you join a new organization. I refer to these meetings as "Meet and Greets". Alternatively, you can always take the initiative to introduce yourself via email. You may not have as much control or flexibility as to when you can have these meetings but you need to ensure you have them. You have to be very deliberate in having such interactions.

The consistency of this level of interaction depends primarily on the relationships that you have with your leaders and on their leadership style. If they are hands-off and prefer a more impersonal approach, getting these meetings to become regular may be close to impossible and ultimately uncomfortable and painful for everyone involved.

If you are in the unfortunate situation of directly reporting to management, which does not like personal interactions, the best thing is to use the meetings you do get with them to advocate for your team. Your most important job in that scenario is to be their voice and escalate any concerns they may have. If in-person meetings are not possible, use the next best means of getting your team's concerns heard.

When you have management that cares about the human impact of their interactions with you, the best thing you can do is have these meetings in person. This will ensure both of you get the most out of your sessions. When you are new to a workplace, it's ideal to ensure that everyone up the leadership chain knows what your role is and who you are. This helps you avoid any unnecessary impediments.

One of the most important conversations I have with management over email or in person is about any matters that impact the organization, especially market forces. For example, if there's something relevant to our industry making headlines in the news, I educate myself on the issue and the potential impact it might have on our organization and take any required steps to counteract the threat. Then, I make sure to inform management of these threats and the steps we've taken to mitigate them or recommendations that need their approval. In an ideal scenario, I would hope that my team brings such matters to me that I can subsequently vet and report upwards if required. However, sometimes that doesn't happen, and it's crucial not to drop the ball and create an information gap that may lead to disastrous effects.

You would hope that meetings with your leaders are productive and filled with mutual presence. That may not always be the case. If you have a cordial relationship with your leader, you may be able to gently and gracefully raise your concerns if they happen to be multitasking during your meeting and you find that distracting from the impact your meeting can have. Asking them if there might be a better time to meet instead may be one approach you take. However, we can all agree that if you don't have a cordial relationship with your leader, you are out of luck and need to focus on influencing the best-case outcomes of your meeting. You need to figure out what kind of leader you have and make any necessary adjustments to your expectations or goals.

My Message to You

Developing your team is a very deliberate exercise. The foundation for successfully developing your team rests on the trust and establishment of the operating principles I opened this chapter with. You and your team can not successfully enjoy the benefits of being part of a high-performing team without TTIPPC (Transparency, Togetherness, Inclusion, Presence, Participation, and Consistency).

Regardless of your efforts and even intentions, sometimes things do not go as well as you hoped. Maybe things can be misspoken, a team member overlooked, or intentions misinterpreted. When these things eventually happen, stepping back, taking a breath, and exercising grace and sound judgment can make a world of difference.

As you navigate the team development process, I encourage you to stay true to yourself, keep an open mind, know and establish your boundaries, and cultivate a lifestyle of endurance to get through the inevitable tough patches. Additionally, make sure you take time to regroup and refocus particularly when you are overwhelmed.

Team development is an exercise in nurturing. The same elements you would use to successfully take care of a beloved family member, pet, or friend who can not take care of themselves are required. As with those examples, taking up such involving roles is hardly ever easy, but they are certainly rewarding.

In this chapter, we focused on team development. The focus was the team members that you hire into your team. However, your team does not work in isolation. Your team has external partners that contribute to the success of your team. Skillfully working together is another part of what makes your team successful. In the next chapter, we will discuss how you can effectively collaborate or influence external contributors to ensure your team succeeds in the workforce.

Chapter 4

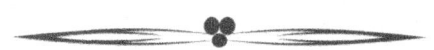

Collaborating with Partners

"The best partnerships aren't dependent on a mere common goal but on a shared path of equality, desire, and no small amount of passion" - Sarah Maclean[41]

In the previous chapter, we focused on developing your team. In this chapter, we will look at how you can successfully collaborate with partners - both external to the organization and internally. Let me let you in on how I see things: my team isn't just the team members who report to

---

[41] Hinga, Juliet. "Partners' Appreciation Cocktail". 2022, October 31. Strathmore University Business School. https://sbs.strathmore.edu/partners-appreciation-cocktail/#:~:text=%E2%80%9CThe%20best%20partnerships%20aren't,of%20passion.%E2%80%9D%20Sarah%20Maclean.

me. My team includes the external and internal parties that help us be successful. This can include vendors, other members of the organization who work closely with us, and individual contractors we interface with.

Effective collaboration includes understanding the dynamics of collaboration, defining roles, making stakeholders "part of the team", maintaining stakeholder relationships, and measuring performance. Let's begin by looking at partnering with external and internal stakeholders.

Partnering with Internal and External Stakeholders

Though internal and external stakeholders can contribute to your team's success, your approach must be different for each. This is because of the unique aspects that come into play because of the technicalities, particularly those of a legal nature. We will take a closer look at those in the subsequent sections. For now, let's focus on aspects of partnering with internal stakeholders.

Internal Stakeholders

When it comes to partnering with internal stakeholders, the first thing you need to do is identify who these internal stakeholders are. You have to have the answer to the following: Who do I have to know, and who needs to know me outside of my team but within the organization?

Once you have the answer, your next move should be to organize some "meet and greets" with the individuals identified. During those meetings, typically 30 minutes long, I ask them several questions, including the following:

> ➤ What's working?
> ➤ What's not working?
> ➤ What's your perception?
> ➤ What are your concerns?
> ➤ Who should I look out for?

If done right, this interaction should be the beginning of a healthy working relationship and open dialogue. Regardless of what I'm informed of, I make sure to temper it with my own opinion, investigation, and an open mind since perception varies. To have a balanced opinion of the facts on the ground, you have to be cautious in your assessment, especially when it comes to your opinions of others based on preconceived notions.

Naturally, you will have to interface with various people in your organization. As an example, in my role in cybersecurity, I needed to have a good working relationship with Internal Audit. Internal auditors will test your controls. They will also make sure that your controls are operating effectively. You need to develop a good working relationship with them. You need to ensure that they know who you are, what controls exist, and what's important to them. Then, you need to partner with them in meeting any deadlines for whatever evidence they need quarterly for financial reports.

External Stakeholders

There will be people, organizations, and other teams that your team needs to collaborate with to get their jobs done. These are your external stakeholders. Some of them may have contracts with your organizations responsible for delivering services to your organization. Their work helps make your team's work effective. In my previous roles, this would be service providers offering their infrastructure for networking, customer support, and vendors of software and hardware solutions that our organization depended on.

Over the years, I found that it was never enough just to know individuals in these organizations for when you needed them to execute our organization's directives. I learned that it was vital we establish ongoing relationships so we could function as one. Forming relationships with external parties also helps you understand what is within their sphere of influence, what isn't, and why. When you have this type of information, you know what to expect from them. You also know what not to expect from them and can make contingency plans accordingly. Let me give you an example:

Once, at a previous employer's, we had an internet service outage at one of our facilities. Ordinarily, one could simply assume that this was due to a problem on our internet service provider's (ISP's) end. When we investigated the matter, we discovered that it had nothing to do with them. A local utility company had mistakenly dug into the fiber optic cables in the road. These cables formed part of the last mile of our internet network, and this damage led to the internet outage we experienced. In light of this information, we knew that our internet service provider was not in any position to rectify the fault. This information allowed us to communicate to our colleagues on the affected site with more accurate and actionable information.

Understanding the nature of the fault was very important to our contractual relationship with the service provider and even the part of the organization they serviced. Without this information that I was able to forward, my colleagues at that site would have gone on to believe that this provider was failing to meet their contractual obligations when it simply wasn't the case.

In situations like the one I've illustrated above, it is never enough to simply say, "The service provider is working on rectifying the problem." No, you need to be transparent and give relevant parties an accurate context for what they are experiencing. Keep this in mind, especially when you were involved in entering into a service agreement with this provider.

If you partner with multiple service providers, you need to ensure these service providers know their boundaries and how to work together for your team's success. It would make your job more effective if you could ensure, for example, that your internet service provider engages effectively with your key hardware providers. This type of relationship may sound irrelevant, but I promise you that there is great value in this, especially when the unexpected happens. During a crisis, the established relationships you've helped foster between your providers can carry you through to the other side.

What's more, if you are incorporating any new team members who need to interface with these external stakeholders, you need to ensure they are properly onboarded to understand the service's scope and the working relationship's current state.

Selecting External Stakeholders

The organization you work at will typically have procedures to contract external stakeholders for any solution your team needs. A common course may begin with a

Request For Information (RFI). This is a structured process that you put out to potential suppliers to assert what they are capable of offering and what you may need from them.

At the same time, you can gauge whether or not you need what they offer. You also want to figure out what would be required or needs to be done if you do need any of their given solutions. This process is essentially a data collection process that will inform your decision-making.

After the RFI, the Request for Proposal (RFP) process will follow. In this process, an RFP document is developed. This document includes details of your requirements as to what you need from a solution or serviceability perspective. It is shared publicly with the goal of suitable suppliers responding in your desired application format with how they can tangibly meet your requirements.

Once you've successfully sourced suitable proposals and determined which service providers can sufficiently meet your requirements and align with your organization's interests, then you move on to the Request For Quotes (RFQ) process. In this process, the main goal is to determine the financial component of any transactions resulting from business being carried out with these external parties.

Ideally, you have a set of criteria that guide your

decision-making processes at each of these three stated phases, similar to the criteria you set out when you are engaged in the hiring process. If you want to find the right fit for external stakeholders, it's crucial to take a thoughtful approach when hiring these third parties because of their potential impact on your team's success. You also have to ensure consistency in the type of information you ask each of your potential stakeholders for. Among the myriad of details you may request from third parties, you should include customer/client reviews and traceable references. Again, this is similar to how you would approach hiring a new employee.

Challenges of Managing External Stakeholders

There are several challenges unique to managing external stakeholders that we need to take a moment to address. These challenges include boundaries and potential conflicts of interest, such as co-employment and confidentiality.

Boundaries

Establishing and maintaining boundaries can be a real challenge in the stakeholder relationship. Every party needs to have a firm grasp on their boundaries as external stakeholders work together with you. Here's an example:

"As a service provider who worked with Tammy's organization, I found her efforts incorporated us into the fold and helped us do a better job. Ordinarily, we would all just go in, do our jobs and get out. Tammy's approach showed us a more efficient way of doing things. You see, there was potential for the ISP, key hardware provider, and application support provider to have conflict at times. Support tickets would often take far longer to resolve, involve unnecessary back and forths and many times these support requests were not adequately attended to. To avoid the blame game, Tammy made sure to link these organizations and facilitate the establishment of working relationships.

Tammy began by encouraging each of these organizations to appoint their service delivery managers to the responsibility of engaging with the other organizations regularly. She advised them to focus their discussions on what was going on within their domain of expertise, what was working and what was not. They also had to be linked so every party was aware of where the handoffs were to ensure mutual accountability, proactivity, and collaboration. What Tammy didn't want was people assigning blame because of any ambiguity.

Ultimately, we realized that the approach Tammy

employed really helped break down the almost adversarial approach some of us had to our fellow providers that we had an overall with. We learned that outside of engaging with this organization, we are competitors but when it comes to dealing with this organization we are actually players on the same team. If the organization succeeds, we all succeed. Tammy's methods of helping us foster relationships with each other helped us see and live the bigger picture."

-Jasper

Conflicts of Interest

In some cases, external stakeholders' resistance in collaborating in serving your organization may be legitimate. This can be challenging for everyone involved. When I have the opportunity to select external providers, I find organizations that do not pose a direct competitive threat to each other. This may not always be possible. In those instances, I communicate to both parties how their engagement with our organization (in particular, the services each provides) is different from the other and should be seen as such. Their job is to figure out how to successfully work together with us while protecting their interests. When each party knows how to "stay in their lane", it is possible to work together without any conflict of interest.

On some occasions, I've had one stakeholder decline to attend certain meetings because a company they perceive as a direct competitor will be in attendance. However, I would often remind them that both parties provide different services to our organization. So while they may compete in other spaces, they did not compete in the scope of my team.

Another issue involving conflicts of interest is the potential for overlap or co-employment. In my leadership style, my goal is to make internal and external parties part of the team as far as is legally and reasonably acceptable. They must have access to all the information that they need to do a great job. It is also necessary that they forge relationships with you and your team that help them accomplish the same. From my experience, this means ensuring they become part of the fold. However, as your organization does not employ them, you can not treat them exactly as your team members. There has to be that difference to accommodate the legal aspect that dictates your relationship with each other.

Confidentiality

As you share information with external parties, the issue of confidentiality is pivotal. The difference in how you interact with these external parties includes withholding confidential, sensitive, or otherwise restricted information that is not in your company's interest to share beyond the confines of your team. Sometimes, this also means restricting information from internal stakeholders that your team may not be able to share with them yet.

Naturally, this filtering of information requires great diligence on your part. When you want to send out emails and other mass types of communication to your team, including external and internal stakeholders, you need to be certain that you aren't sharing anything that you shouldn't.

Overcoming the Challenges

From experience, I've learned that the key to overcoming many challenges, such as conflicts of interest, boundary infringements, and confidentiality issues, boils down to one main aspect of great leadership: great communication. You have to ensure that you communicate clearly and concisely. You also have to ensure that your team members operate similarly and that you select external parties with well-established and supportive communication protocols.

In one instance, a hardware and software supplier expressed apprehension about joining us at a team-building event. Again, this was because of the presence of another of our suppliers that provided us with a networking solution. I alleviated her concerns because there was a clearly defined scope of service and solution delivery for each of them. The underlying understanding was also that each needed to stay in their lane to continue working with us in such a setup.

Defining Roles

If stakeholders who are integral to your team succeed, then the team succeeds as a unit. However, if that stakeholder fails, then the team fails as a unit. One crucial aspect of positioning yourself for success with these stakeholders is clearly defining roles. Though we briefly touched on the importance of defining roles and responsibilities concerning boundaries for third parties, we will take a moment to take a closer look at defining roles specifically. What I've found particularly useful in identifying and defining roles are RACI charts, the shared accountability matrix, and the contracts that govern the solution or service they offer. Let's take a look at the first one.

RACI Chart

A RACI ("Responsible, Accountable, Consult and Inform") chart is a diagram used in project management for defining team member's roles[42].

---

[42] Landau, Peter. "How to Make a RACI Chart for a Project (With Example)". 2022, September 9. Project Manager. https://www.projectmanager.com/blog/how-to-make-a-raci-chart-for-a-project-with-example

With the aid of a RACI chart, you can plot down the following:

➢ The roles and responsibilities that you've identified
➢ The tasks and deliverables scheduled
➢ Assignments of these deliverables, tasks, and milestones against the individuals held responsible in their respective roles.

Here's an example:

Task	Vendor Mgmt	Executive Sponsor	Business Owner	Legal	IT & Info Sec
Identify standard terms & conditions for contract	C	-	R/A	C	C
Negotiate contract	C	C	R/A	C	-
Review final draft against standards	C	C	C	R/A	C
Execute contract	I	R/A	I	I	I
Store contract in contract management system	R/A	-	I	-	-
Assign contract owner	R/A	I	I	I	I
Integrate new vendor through onboarding process	C	I	R/A	-	C

Credit Source: https://vendorcentric.com/single-post/using-RACI-charts-to-strengthen-third-party-management/

In the example above, you'll note the following letters that make up the word "RACI", implying the four main aspects of the chart. With these elements, you can easily plot, track, and communicate who is responsible for a task, accountable for ensuring it happens, who needs to be consulted, and who simply needs to be informed. You will note in our example that your head of department will need to be informed of these developments, whilst you will be held accountable if your team doesn't end up contracting those selected external parties. And, of course, procurement is responsible for ensuring all these processes happen in the first place.

Knowing aspects such as who should be held accountable, informed, or consulted streamlines the whole collaboration process so you never end up spinning your wheels. Crafting an effective RACI diagram also requires incorporating the relevant parties in your organization, according to your organization's hierarchical structure. In the above example, we have the head of the department, the procurement manager, and you - the team leader, as part of your organizational structure that is relevant to this RACI chart. These individuals happen not to be in the same reporting unit.

When it comes to managing teams, treating these interactions as projects and using frameworks like the RACI diagram can help you sustain a level of clarity that could otherwise be difficult to sustain. The more clarity you can offer all parties, the less opportunity there is for confusion or a mismanaged outcome.

Shared Accountability Matrix

A shared accountability matrix is a chart that you can use to convey the service level agreements the external parties are required to meet. The shared accountability matrix goes hand in hand with the RACI chart as it also defines what part of the relationship each party is responsible for. With its proper usage, the supplier, the client, and the customer all know what is expected of themselves and each other.

The Service Contract

When you have documentation like this helping you navigate your relationships with internal and external parties, they offer another great benefit, especially useful when you find yourself working in an organization with a culture of blaming and finger-pointing. In that particular scenario, these documents and reverting to the terms and conditions outlined in the contract can help you convey to the team any clarifications when there are misunderstandings regarding contractual obligations.

Contract development can feel daunting because of all the legalese you have to wade through. If a time comes when other members of your organization or even you are questioning the performance of any of your contractors, reverting to their contract can be helpful for your response to them. In such a scenario, it is your most important reference document because it should easily show if they are failing to meet their contractual commitments.

Of course, if a stakeholder fails to meet their contractual obligations and negatively affects the success of your team, this means they are in breach of their contract. Such a breach could warrant a premature termination of the contract or a subsequent decline to renew your contract when the time comes. The decision the most responsible party would make would have to include several considerations in the organization's best interest, particularly financial implications.

Making Stakeholders "Part of the Team"

I've already shared with you that there are certain types of sensitive information that internal and external stakeholders that make up part of your team may not be privy to. Just as they also have confidential information within their organization and should be respected as such. These types of sensitive information could include anything connected to an ongoing investigation or lawsuit that's been filed.

That said, it bears repeating that making these stakeholders part of your team is sometimes a delicate balance. You have to straddle the line between ensuring you don't create a scenario of "co-employment" and not create such a distance that these stakeholders feel their status as non-employees presents unique barriers that impede their effective performance. Insurance and compensation-related concerns are additional aspects you need to keep in mind as you orchestrate these relationships. Some organizations are very strict about the type of corporate events their representatives can attend at your organization. They may inform you that their representatives can not attend your holiday parties and or certain diversity and inclusion events. Other organizations may have no qualms with this. As this varies, you need to be well-versed in the rules of engagement with every stakeholder you work with.

When the rules allow, I prefer it when these stakeholders can spend time with us in such informal settings. These are opportunities to develop relationships that will ultimately impact their service delivery, acquaint them with key players, get them up to date with what's happening, and integrate them into our operations.

Making stakeholders part of the team also needs a

healthy exercise of discernment. Timing is paramount. If, for example, your organization is acquiring another, you may not include that new addition until the deal is closed. However, once the paperwork goes through, your job is to ensure that these new team members have everything they need to do a great job.

As a leader, you will have access to information that many don't. The elements of discretion and good timing regarding transparency come into play again when disseminating information. You must only share information when you are allowed to and apply the necessary filters based on your audience at a given time when you can not. These filters aren't just in the case of direct in-person conversation but any type of written or oral communication.

On the other hand, representatives of other organizations working with your team have the responsibility to honor their organizations' codes of conduct and expectations to avoid any possibility of exposure and violations of their employment contracts as they work with us.

Maintaining Stakeholder Relationships

The essence of maintaining stakeholder relationships is pegged on the qualities we discussed of a great leader in

Chapter 1 and the operating principles (TTIPPC) we looked at in Chapter 3. You will need to ensure that these stakeholders also absorb principles (transparency, togetherness, inclusion, presence, participation, and consistency) that you expect all your team members to embody.

If you intend to have regular meetings with your stakeholders, ensure that you consistently maintain that arrangement. At the beginning of a relationship with a service provider, you may wish to have weekly incident review meetings for a time.

Weekly and Monthly Meetings

If you have these weekly meetings in the early stages of your working relationship with stakeholders, you would want to ask the questions like:

1. What happened this week? Anything weird?
2. What's still open?
3. What do you need help with?

After that, you have a monthly operational meeting discussing trends throughout the past couple of months. In those meetings, you want to determine if they meet our service-level agreements from a target perspective.

You also need to ensure that there is an agenda for each meeting, stay on track with any commitments you made to them, and document action items from previous meetings and expectations against those action items. The consistency of the messaging, your preparation for these meetings, and showing up are part of your success in maintaining these stakeholder relationships.

Now, these meetings are not just about what these stakeholders (whether internal or external) are doing or not doing. These meetings also afford you the chance to share with them what your team is doing as well.

I like to share with our partners that they are welcome to tell me what our team is doing wrong or if our team needs to do something differently. These partners must know these meetings are collaborative and bidirectional. You need to help them understand that either side may have an opportunity to do better, and voicing their feedback is what can help attain the mutual success we strive for. These meetings can not be just about what the team is or is not doing well.

Creating this atmosphere helps you build that equity and equality for healthy and robust teams. I have found that accepting candor and being willing to give the same in return is the most productive approach. This may look like you are not pulling any punches as you convey the results of a survey carried out about how the organization is doing. If a customer satisfaction survey brings back disheartening results, I am sure to share that feedback with our stakeholders, so they have a precise impression of any concerns our team has regarding our collective contribution to those results. In some cases, when the feedback seems invalid, particularly if it appears to be skewed or unreasonable, I may opt not to share unsatisfactory customer satisfaction data.

Quarterly Business Reviews

Thereafter, you have a quarterly business review. As the name suggests, these happen three times, four times a year. There, you talk about things like the health of the relationship between the organization and the external partner. You make sure all bills are getting paid on time. You follow up on anything coming up that they might need your help with. In large organizations, these meetings are fairly high-level, involving the organization's higher-ranking leadership.

Managing Perception

Sometimes, it's your responsibility to manage perceptions related to the stakeholders. When you receive feedback pointing to unmet expectations and poor performance, you can communicate with your team or organization members with these concerns regarding their validity. Since you are the one who owns the contract with them, and has access to the RACI chart and shared accountability matrix, you are in the perfect position because you can see the broader picture. In that scenario, you can then share with the relevant parties the details they are missing or misinterpreting. You would also have to put measures in place to safeguard from these misconceptions happening again.

However, if the concerns brought to light are indeed valid, you need to take these up with the relevant stakeholders and present the matter before them with the relevant backing details, data, and documentation where possible.

I am delighted to share that I've had outstanding results in managing perception within my teams. My stakeholders would feel so part of the team that when quarterly meetings were scheduled, they would often make efforts to attend in person, even if they were based out of town. Often, they would become so a part of us that other people in our organization knew who they were, too. The stakeholders would also try to carve out time to engage with the direct liaisons from within the organization outside of office hours in a non-threatening environment to strengthen the relationship. These individuals became so ingrained in our team that they truly were an extension of our team. We knew that as long as they were in those organizations, our interests were given the attention they deserved. This is something that you can master, too.

The most delightful benefit of this level of engagement was that you can engage with these stakeholders with as much candor as you need when you need it. You will also notice how they will go above and beyond to ensure they do not disappoint you or the team. Because, in this case, they would not only be disappointing a client but "colleagues" who have vouched for them time and time again. When it comes to negotiations or situations that call for your organization to make cuts in costs, this established trust can also work in both your favor in arriving at win-win situations and mutual understanding.

Measuring Performance

To ensure both internal and external stakeholders are holding up to their ends of the bargain, you need to measure performance and put a course of action in place when they fall short. Now, in the case of internal stakeholders, you do not have much power over certain outcomes. The most you can do is exert a level of influence in the direction you hope matters go. So, in this section, we will focus on the elements of measuring performance and remediation associated with external stakeholders that you manage.

There are contractual obligations that have to be met by external stakeholders. We talked about this in earlier sections of this chapter. If those contractual obligations are not being met, there are times when there can be penalties applied from a financial perspective. There can be rebates because the service level was missed. So, measuring performance is primarily about holding your external stakeholders accountable for what they signed up to do for the organization.

To effectively hold your external partners accountable, you need to establish expectations clearly defined in the contract. A service level agreement without this is inadequate. With these expectations presented, you can measure the performance using a performance matrix. This performance matrix is not a document that you alone have access to. You need to ensure that the criteria for their performance are easily accessible to the relevant partner. This transparency and visibility of your performance criteria is a reasonable effort on your part since you are not only on the same team, but you want your service provider to succeed. As I've already stated, if they win, you win. Making sure they know what "winning" looks like to you, gives them the advantage that they need to perform accordingly.

Sometimes, performance may fall outside of the desired range. In those instances, you need to be on top of it and communicate with your provider. You also need to institute a "Go Green" plan to help them get back to an acceptable level of performance. When you have your monthly or quarterly, you need to highlight where their performance stands (green, yellow, or red). If the situation is problematic, you need to find out the root cause of the problem. If the problem was a random hiccup, the remediation would be different from that which is systemic. As you unearth the issues, you need to find out what needs to be done to fix them, who will do it, and if this type of problem will be expected. With all this data, you then need to do both trending and validation.

Trending

When a partner is not performing up to par, you may wish to get metrics back from them weekly instead of monthly or quarterly. This approach helps you to identify any patterns at a more granular level.

If a service provider fails to meet their contractual agreements for three months in a row, you need to find out what's going on. Did they over-commit? Are they experiencing resource constraints that you are not aware of? Have developments in your organization created hurdles for them, impeding their previously stellar performance? Sometimes, the performance matrix can trend in the right direction. Again, this will help you stay on top of the dynamics affecting your team's success.

When they are not, you need to put into place a "Go Green " plan with the goal of the stakeholder getting back on track and in the green zone of your performance matrix. This often includes collaborating with them on an action plan - similar to the "performance improvement plan" I talked about when we looked at improving employee performance.

Validation

You need verifiable data backing up any claims you make about poor performance or breach of service of your partners. That is where the concept of "validation" is key. If you present them with any concerns about their performance, you need verifiable data to present to them, otherwise it is simply conjecture and hearsay. If the matter eventually leads to your desire to terminate the contract, this lack of data will work against you and may even open up your organization to liabilities and lawsuits.

If you do not have the data, the relationship built on transparency and trust is easily challenged. You need to present the matter to them and request their cooperation to dispel any claims emanating from your organization. If, for example, your provider in question offers you call center support and you received claims that calls to them are hardly answered, you would ask them to show you call logs to help diagnose the problem.

If they are in a position to share this type of data with you, you can work together to rectify the problem. If they inform you that they, too, do not have any data to check these claims, your next step would be to request them to make efforts to attain data that you can still use to dispel these claims in some way. If they are uncooperative, then you have an additional concern to address. If they are cooperative but still lack the data, the action plan they can put together with your guidance could include detailed call logs and summaries for you. If they establish these measures, and the problem is successfully identified, they are 50% closer to solving the problem with you as a team.

I mentioned the perception issue earlier, and that comes into play again. Without data, perception is reality. In any action plan, an attempt also needs to be made to address any perceptions of failure that may have arisen from these incidents. Again, it goes back to having data. You will need that data if the situation further deteriorates and to make an effective go-green plan.

If we take a moment to look at the concept of validation when there is no data, trust is a big component of getting to the other side of this situation. It means you must have mutual trust. If the other party can not be trusted, making genuine headway in this area may be close to impossible. I would not like for you to end up in such a situation. One way you can help yourself steer clear of such is by hiring external parties that are proven trustworthy and have a high sense of integrity and quality control.

There will be times when you inherit a team and its stakeholders that would not be your first choice. When faced with stakeholders that are a mismatch for you in terms of integrity, trustworthiness, and ethics, if you are unable to disengage from them, you need to step up. Where they offer you no data, your team has to start working to compile detailed and relevant data from available sources. Ideally, you would want to work with them to agree on what measurable results they need to supply you with to quash any claims against the provider's performance. However, if the provider is uncooperative, you can use these as the facts at hand. You are then seen to be leading with facts and not charged emotions. When you do that, your data defines reality and not unsubstantiated perception.

If the partner can install a system to get these measurable results, that would be ideal. However, if they aren't, even manual collection would have to suffice. It's better than nothing. If this problem is ongoing, there's clearly a lack of some element holding them accountable in that area. If you notice that these challenges are ongoing without effectively being addressed from the partner's side, you now need to start assessing the terms of termination of the contract that governs your relationship with this business. You will need to know the terms for early termination, who can terminate the contract, and what evidence is required to accomplish this termination.

If you notice these issues early in your engagement with this partner, I strongly encourage you to keep procurement and the legal department abreast of these developments. This can allow them to become acquainted with the situation and prepare for it if the issue escalates into a case of termination. I would also encourage you to have meticulous documentation and data to back up and defend your decision to terminate a given contract. Detailed documentation may look like chronologically presented events, actions taken or not taken with any necessary data attached. You must keep that evidence trail of why you are in this situation and always focus on the facts, not emotions. There is usually a time boundary when you enter into such a contract. In most cases, you can't get out of it unless you pay a lot of money to break your contract early or because they are in breach of delivering the services that they committed to.

My Message to You

The bottom line is that internal and external stakeholders are part of your team. They are an extension of your team. As such, they should be afforded as much support, grace, interaction, and camaraderie as they can within the legal framework your organization and their organization allows. As you monitor their performance, always respond in a way that supports your mutual continued efforts. As you would with excellent performance from within your team, don't forget to share positive feedback with them and their organizations to foster an ongoing positive relationship. Even just a sincere "thank you!" can go a long way. It's simple but often forgotten. In this chapter, we focussed on the dynamics of influencing and working with external and internal stakeholders. In the next chapter, we will focus on the bigger picture of how you can sustain a high-performing team - your reportees, internal stakeholders, and external stakeholders included. Putting together a great team is just part of the solution. Making this team sustainably perform well is the longer and even more challenging part of the equation you must master. So, let me show you how you can achieve that.

Chapter 5

Sustaining a High Performing Team

"Whether they stem from business or personal situations, our relationships are what support us, connect us, and allow us to progress in all aspects of our lives." — Michelle Tillis Lederman, 11 Laws of Likability[43]

It's one thing assembling a team of great people working together on a common goal over some time. It's another matter entirely sustaining optimal performance over months, years, and even decades. Up to this chapter, we've spent time understanding the dynamics impacting high-

---

[43] GoodReads. "Whether they stem from business or personal situations, our relationships are what support us, connect us, and allow us to progress in all aspects of our lives."

— Michelle Tillis Lederman, 11 Laws of Likability". Building Relationships Quotes. (n.d.). https://www.goodreads.com/quotes/tag/building-relationships

performing teams, assembling the right team members, developing your team, and collaborating with partners. In this Chapter, we need to talk about how you keep that great team consistently performing at its level-best throughout the different seasons that may come your way.

From my experience, there are some unique characteristics that teams that sustain high performance have that the rest do not. We shall explore those first. Then, we will look at maintaining alignment with the team's goals and objectives, understanding your team members' career aspirations, providing development and performance feedback, motivating team members, managing transformational change, and dealing with stress before giving my closing message to you. Let's take a look at the characteristics of high-performing teams.

Characteristics of High-Performing Teams

In Chapter 1, I shared with you the qualities I believe make a great leader, many of which also make a great team member. When it comes to the matter of sustainability, a unique set of characteristics comes into play, too. Time, friction, internal turmoil, and external tension work upon us as individuals and as a team, we need more to keep us working together and enjoying it.

Grace, safety, reciprocity, and resilience are four characteristics I've discovered as pivotal to sustaining high-performing teams and the relationships underpinning them. Think about it for a moment. You don't even have to think about your work environment to identify these characteristics. Your best friend, favorite cousin, mentor, and relative. Any healthy and long-lasting relationship is or at least should be built on these four elements.

Grace

You may be familiar with the word "grace" from different contexts, most likely religious. Yes, that's the original context from which I borrowed this concept. If you are unfamiliar with the term, here's a definition that might help you grasp the concept, outside of a religious or spiritual context:

"Grace is unconditional love toward a person who does not deserve it." - Paul Zahl[44]

Perhaps in the concept of work relationships, the phrase "unconditional love" may sound out of place. How about - within the work context - we look at it as "

---

[44] Holcomb, Justin. "What Is Grace? Bible Definition and Christian Quotes". Wiki. Christianity.com. 2022, August 2. https://www.christianity.com/wiki/christian-terms/what-is-grace.html

generously making room for one another's 'humanity' and occasional weaknesses? That is the bottom line of what grace is all about. None of us is perfect. Despite our best efforts, at some point, we will fail someone - even if that someone is just yourself. When that day comes when we come face to face with our failures, you and I need a healthy serving of some grace.

That said, as a leader, you must give your team members some grace when needed. You must also model that behavior so much that your team members consistently extend the same to others. Lastly, there will be days when you need to direct that grace toward yourself too.

Here is a story - though a tragic one - that can help illustrate the concept of grace further:

An unexpected tragedy happened at a previous workplace, which was a very stressful environment. On an ordinary work day, during the regular day's hustle and bustle, one of the company's finance professionals died in the office building's stairwell.

I can't imagine the sorrow that his family and loved ones must have felt when they learned of his sudden passing. However, I do know the impact his sudden loss on company premises had on us employees. As his colleagues, we mourned his loss. Naturally, colleagues grieved, particularly those who were close to him.

Thankfully, the organization's leadership recognized the significance of our colleague's passing. For the most affected, they relaxed some deadlines. They also offered free counseling for those who felt they needed it.

Looking back, I think the company's efforts were truly admirable. I hope the counseling sessions were enough for each person and not limited in such a way that someone truly needing them didn't feel sufficiently assisted through their grief and trauma.

I recall many incidents that needed a healthy dose of grace for the other party or myself to get through. Particularly in matters to do with tragedy, loss, and other destabilizing personal experiences, grace is crucial. People are not machines. There is no way the average human being can deliver their best when their world is crumbling underneath their feet. To expect the best from them regardless is insensitive at worst and wishful thinking at the very least.

When I've had reportees unable to perform because life threw them a curveball, I've sat and discussed the way forward, the different accommodations they may need for the time being, and crafted plans to ensure the team remains productive. Sometimes this meant other team members had to shoulder more responsibility for as long as was reasonable.

There is one caveat about dispensing and receiving grace that I know of. Grace has to be genuine for the other party to receive it as intended. Perhaps you've been in a scenario where someone demonstrated kindness at face value, but when you looked into it, you discovered their efforts were self-serving and somewhat deceptive. Naturally, your trust in them and their motives going forward must have waned.

Giving yourself grace as the leader is synonymous with giving yourself permission to step back and assess the situation that you're in. Understand how that situation impacts you. Assess yourself and figure out what you're going to do about the situation now. You can't do this indefinitely. You need to figure out a permanent solution. Even so, you cannot beat yourself up because you don't have all the answers right now.

Here's a story that touches upon the matter of grace for yourself as a leader:

"It was the middle of a week-long team-building

session. Tammy was quite busy when she heard the sad news that her mother had suffered a fall. Now, at the time Tammy was away in New Jersey and her mother was back in Pennsylvania. She was a one-and-a-half-hour drive away.

That said, she immediately communicated her situation and made arrangements to attend to her mother's health. As soon as she could, Tammy returned to the team building sessions ensuring that the team knew that they too were important to her"

- Sonny

Let me offer you my most vulnerable story about giving yourself grace as a leader:

People that have worked with me consider me a strong leader. My performance and capabilities speak for themselves, so I would agree. However, at one workplace, I had a very challenging experience. I found myself constantly in defense mode for my team concerning the organization's leadership as external forces came and disrupted business as usual.

During one meeting with my team, I was overwhelmed, and I broke down and cried. This emotional breakdown was something I could have mercilessly beat myself up for but I realized I deserved some grace. In *fairness, the grace my team extended to me when and after this incident happened was also what helped transform this incident from a traumatic one into a growth experience. You see, members of my team approached me and shared how witnessing my vulnerability enabled them to see my humanity. They knew how strong I was from months of leadership, but they had never seen the side that everyone has that we sometimes feel the need to hide or suppress.*

Lastly, giving others grace and adopting a stance of kindness and forgiveness may sometimes open you up to being taken advantage of. To avoid that, you need to be careful. Before engaging with anyone, you need to establish your boundaries and expectations upfront. These have to fall within your organization's code of conduct and be reasonably attainable by most people with the capacity that you hired for. In addition, you need to know what is unacceptable to you in advance. You may have tighter or looser boundaries than others. You may be able to experience more behaviors that someone else would immediately find unacceptable.

When confronted with repeated boundary violations, disrespect, and unacceptable behavior, it's your job to terminate that experience. Giving grace should not and must not make you become someone else's doormat. So, know your limits and live by them.

So, when that day comes, you need to direct grace at yourself, too. Instead of beating yourself up for whatever you know you could have handled differently, you need to stop, **breathe**, and treat yourself the way you hope someone kind would treat you. Then, when you are ready, conclude it with an actionable plan.

Safety

Safety is *"...the condition of being safe from undergoing or causing hurt, injury, or loss"*[45]. Have you ever taken a moment to analyze the most enjoyable relationships in your workplace or even life in general? I bet you'll note that these relationships are also quite safe. You and the other party can trust one another to express concerns, anger, fear, and other negative emotions without fear that you'll lose the connection. The stability allows you to flourish and focus on the work. When you manage your work and attempt to do that in a volatile environment, the added stress of treading such a tightrope can keep your hair on edge.

Albeit, at the beginning stages of team development,

---

[45] Merriam-Webster. "Safety". Dictionary. (n.d.). https://www.merriam-webster.com/dictionary/safety

especially in the forming, storming, and norming stages, safety is something you are all learning to cultivate. Once the team successfully transitions to the performing stage, safety needs to be characteristic of your team.

Reciprocity

Can you think of one healthy and lasting relationship of yours where there is no reciprocity? Neither can I. Reciprocity is *"the quality or state of being reciprocal: mutual dependence, action, or influence"*[46]. Giving and taking needs to be bidirectional for you to all enjoy the benefits of being in an effective team. The leader and team members all have countless opportunities to give and receive.

You may have experienced a scenario where you only give in a specific relationship. At first, you may find it effortless, but one day, this constant giving leaves you depleted and possibly even resentful. Exercising reciprocity means pouring into each other. Let's keep in mind that some people are naturally more thoughtful and considerate than others. With those types of people, it's best to diplomatically gently nudge them when they need a reminder to exercise more giving than receiving.

---

[46] Merriam-Webster. "Reciprocity". Dictionary. (n.d.). https://www.merriam-webster.com/dictionary/reciprocity

Resilience

Resilience is *"... the process and outcome of successfully adapting to difficult or challenging life experiences, especially through mental, emotional, and behavioral flexibility and adjustment to external and internal demands....".*

No matter who you are, an unexpected day will arrive. Something that you didn't see coming will present itself before you, and you will have no other choice but to deal with it, or else it will deal with you.

This unexpected event could be at your workplace or in your personal life. The impact of whatever challenge you're facing can seep into all the other spheres of your life, depending on how you handle it or how impactful the situation is to you. A new boss at an otherwise stellar company could make your life more challenging than you would like. A diagnosis, illness, or natural disaster can quite literally throw you off-course, leaving you wondering if you still have what it takes to get the job done, let alone get out of bed in the morning. The list of potential challenges is endless. We could each easily fill in blank pages for our individual experiences.

If we are observant, we can easily see how easy it is for some people to bounce back from tragedies; for others, the same event could leave them permanently derailed. Our internal resources are unique for each of us. Knowing what you have to work with, how you handle chaos or unprecedented events, and putting together a plan for when that happens can help you get through it faster and, most importantly, come out of it with growth instead of just new trauma.

Having resilience also means being proactive in fixing your challenges or those you are involved in. If your team fails to deliver and causes a knock-on effect of problems for adjourning teams, leading to challenges for them, too, the first thing that's important for you and everyone to understand is that if you don't start to fix this problem immediately, the problem will compound. If that problem compounds, it may reach the point of no return, leading to consequences that could jeopardize your team and even your role in it. In such a situation, you need to buckle up and face the situation.

Accept the predicament you've found yourself in and figure out who you need to have conversations with, prepare a plan for repairing the situation, apologize and acknowledge your role in the problem, and institute that plan for repairing the situation. If you are given a second chance, your job is to work towards deserving it and reinstate your credibility. Coming back from such things is not easy, so accepting that it will take hard work is part of the journey towards rectifying the problem.

Maintaining Alignment of the Team's Goals and Objectives

It is significantly easier to stay focused on your team's goals and objectives in an atmosphere of grace, safety, reciprocity, and resilience. This combination helps your team maintain high performance. Though maintaining ongoing alignment of team goals and objectives leans heavily towards your organization's personnel department, it is still an aspect of team leadership that great leaders in any part of an organization pay attention to. Maintaining alignment of team goals and objectives involves setting attainable goals and objectives, monitoring performance periodically, and sustaining healthy communication. To maintain goals and objectives, we need to first establish those attainable goals and objectives. Let's take a look at setting goals and objectives.

Setting Team Goals and Objectives

If you are not at the very top of your organization's leadership hierarchy, and head one team or division in your organization, then the goals you designate for your team will stem from the organization's overall goals. Goals and objectives cascade from the top.

You will typically set your goals and objectives at the beginning of the performance year. In most cases, this is the calendar year. In other cases, it may align with your organization's fiscal year, if it is different. At that point, you need to fully understand the company's goals and objectives. This is another reason I ensure that my team and I understand the organization's business and what it does in all its major divisions. You must ensure your understanding is thorough enough to know the broader and primary goals. If your organization is a business, the top goals will naturally be of financial importance, such as revenue generation and market share gained by the end of that year. As you develop your team's goals, you must map them back to the company's primary and broader goals and objectives. This helps the team understand how they are helping the company achieve those business goals.

Being transparent with your team regarding how you arrived at the goals and objectives you set for them helps your team move away from an insular or siloed perspective. They get to see how they fit into the bigger picture. From my experience in the tech sector, it's common to see people hyper-focused on their skills and deliverables without understanding their impact on the grand scheme of things.

The more you can tie your individual team's goals and objectives to the bigger picture, the more the linkage is apparent between what you want your team to do and how that will enable the company to meet its goals. So, you must do that initial goal setting in the very beginning, at the start of the year. Then, routinely monitor team top priorities derived from your goals and objectives monthly during your group meetings.

You may be wondering how you can ensure you've got great goals and objectives. One useful and popular framework that you may already know of that's invaluable for conceptualizing the elements that go into crafting effective goals is called "SMART".

Getting S.M.A.R.T.

"SMART" stands for **S**pecific, **M**easurable, **A**chievable, **R**ealistic, and **T**imely[47]. You're likely to have success with goals that are structured using a "SMART" framework. Let's dive into the framework:

- "**Specific**" goals are direct, focused, and clear.
- "**Measurable**": It's hard to achieve something when

---

[47] Corporate Finance Institute. "SMART Goals". Management. Corporate Finance Institute. 2023.
https://corporatefinanceinstitute.com/resources/management/smart-goal/

you aren't measuring it. After all, how do you know when you've finally achieved it or if you are falling behind along the way and need to correct the course?
- **"Achievable"**: It's unproductive and unfair to set goals for your team that are simply impossible. That's why you've got to ask yourself if your goal is attainable given the factors and context that your team has to work with at that time.
- **"Realistic"**: Even if a goal is achievable, you need to consider how realistic that goal is in terms of probability and practicality.
- **"Timely"**: When it comes to great goal setting, everything important is mapped out. You know when you will reach each milestone and the ultimate output, with stated inputs. If you need your team to accomplish specific tasks by a given deadline, you need to ensure they have this presented and factored into the goals and objectives they set.

When you set SMART goals at the beginning of your organization's year, you need to monitor progress at every team meeting you have once a month. That's the "top priorities" your team needs to stay on top of and report on during each team meeting. These are derived from the goals that you set. In my case, I would make a point of commenting on these top priorities during these group meetings. I aimed to remind everyone how the efforts we made and the tasks we were committed to tied back to the organization's broader goals. So, regardless of whatever project or projects our team focused on at a given time, we were consistent at taking our attention to the overall or corporate vantage point.

It's also important to pay attention to the goals and objectives your team members set for themselves. You can do this through quarterly and bi-annual meetings that you have with your team members on a one-to-one basis. Your attention in these sessions would need to be on measuring and assessing how much each of them has accomplished towards the goals they set and how you can help them do better. Helping them do better means taking time during these seasons to learn what impacted their outcome. If they only achieved partial success in a given period, you need to find out why. What were their challenges or barriers? Are there any new risks that came in that may have prevented them from achieving their objectives? Perhaps new external factors emerged, shifting the organization's interests and, in turn, your team member's efforts. You need to have this conversation, figure out what's going on, and help them get back on track.

These monthly commentaries and reports on top

priorities during group meetings, the quarterly and bi-annual meetings with individual team members, and other impromptu meetings that require us to pay attention to any goals provide consistency in checking in and resetting goals if necessary.

The end of the year will require a final meeting where we conclusively review each team member's efforts toward their individual goals and a group meeting to collectively assess the team's as well. It's all about assessing what everyone said they would do and if they did it. If there are any gaps, we need to know what, where they are, and why they exist. A lack of gaps could even signify that the individual or team accomplished every goal despite challenges.

It's worth noting that how you approach these engagements is as important, if not more so, than the mechanics of it all. When working with people, the adage that "you attract more bees with honey than vinegar" rings true. Being a hard and overbearing taskmaster may seem effective, but it doesn't truly help your team. I've found that sitting with everyone and showing them how the impact of their efforts relates to the overall organization's success and then routinely measuring their efforts is the best type of "honey". Being a bully or allowing yourself to be perceived as a bully is counterproductive.

This process is essentially a cycle that requires constant communication. As you work through the goal setting at the beginning of the year, maintain consistency of review meetings during the year, and hold final review meetings at its end, you'll start your next year at the top of this cycle. Since each team member's annual performance may impact whether or not they receive a performance award, it's a good idea to encourage them to consistently produce their best to be merit-worthy of such benefits. If they aren't performing well, it's a good idea to keep them updated in terms of whether that takes them out of the running for financial benefits. I highlight this because you don't want them to find it as some sort of surprise when their performance indicates the increasing unlikelihood of it happening in the first place.

Understanding Team Members' Career Aspirations

One important aspect of maintaining the high performance of your team is understanding what their passions and dreams are. Then you need to work with each member toward achieving those aspirations while also furthering the organization's vision. If you can successfully align the individual's passions with the organization's mission and vision, you have a magical combination, and great things are bound to happen. This is another reason why those one-to-one meetings are crucial for everyone. Your team members can be invited to be vulnerable and open about their aspirations, goals, and career desires in those settings.

I've already explained how I conduct these one-to-one meetings in Chapter 3: Developing Your Team. However, here, I would like to outline some of the important questions during one-to-one meetings that help you unearth how you can successfully support each team member towards realizing their best lives. Essentially, these questions are the same questions that help me to assist my team members in establishing an effective development plan:

- *How are you doing?*
- *Are there things you want to accomplish that you would like me to know of or opportunities you would like to try?*
- *What are your career aspirations, or is your desire to stay in this role or field for your whole career?*
- *Would you like to try a different role in the company?*
- *Is there a training that you would like to attend?*

The key to this process being successful lies in this

being an employee-led and leader-supported initiative. If the employee doesn't share their aspirations, you can't help them achieve them. Each employee is essentially responsible for the trajectory of their career. All you and I can do as leaders is create an enabling and supportive environment (and guidance) to help them achieve their desired success.

The questions above determine "who" the employee is, what they want to do (especially if it is different from what they are doing right now), and what we need to do to help them get there. This is a bi-directional exchange that depends on the openness and candidness of the team members for it to be most effective.

It's possible to over-step, and that quality of great leaders - "self-reflection", comes in handy at this point. Giving a team member advice or suggestions about the direction they can take in their careers is fine. What's problematic is that they insist on taking their careers in a direction that they may not be prepared to invest in. That's overstepping your boundaries as a leader and may lead to resentment. Don't force your team members, particularly on issues outside of your domain of control. Your team members need to each own their own development plans.

Ideally, what you would want is a member of your

team coming with information about a training program that they would like to take, how attending it would positively impact their deliverables in their role as a team, and how you and the organization can participate in them using this opportunity to be more successful. Alternatively, a team member that expresses their interest in advancing in whatever role they are in will be on the top of my mind when I come across an opportunity that aligns with their aspirations. If a team member intends to take the leadership route and shares their aspirations with me, then I carve out time to coach them when possible. The support they receive is the support they request based on their expressed needs. It is important to articulate this to each team member to avoid misunderstanding expectations. Someone who never implemented the development plan that you helped them craft may come to you in disappointment at the end of a year when they simply didn't put in the work to make their plan work or didn't pay attention to changing variables and didn't adjust accordingly.

I encourage members of my team to take the initiative. I need them to find resources for their advancement or ask me to help them if they need that support. I am happy to coach them or even help them practice for specific leadership roles and whatever else they need, but they need to drive this engagement.

Sometimes, I find it more beneficial for my team members if I assign them a mentor. Depending on your organization, there may be a mentorship program that aids in that area, whether by finding the employee a mentor that's internal or external to the organization. Outside of these organization-led mentorship opportunities, it is crucial to encourage your team to network and build their professional support system. No matter how great a boss anyone has, having a formal mentorship relationship with someone who's not your boss is important. Websites like LinkedIn can help with that. Encourage your team to have a polished, completed, and up-to-date LinkedIn profile or whatever industry-specific digital presence that makes sense.

Providing Development and Performance Feedback

As you've probably noted, constant communication is part of effective leadership and great team performance. As stated already, you don't want any of your team to experience surprises because of your lack of feedback regarding their development and performance. You need to give both positive and constructive feedback in a timely fashion.

So, this means conveying positive commentary on collective and individual performance when it happens. Even if it's a simple yet sincere "Thank you", that can go a long way to conveying a sense of validation and appreciation. It also means not holding back any factual feedback that may be considered negative. Negative feedback, if constructive, can be as beneficial and effective as positive feedback.

Through opening up channels to receive input from your team about their individual performance and development, you also facilitate them expressing and using their voice. Every team member needs to know they have the option of voicing out their concerns and comments as it pertains to their performance and that of their team.

The "how" of doing something is as important as the "what". You and your team need to be intimately familiar with this aspect of performance. It is also worth bringing up when you give feedback to individual team members, especially when other team members, organizations, or third parties bring up concerns relating to this. Your team or specific members can meet the goals and objectives agreed upon within the timeline set but manage to accomplish that whilst alienating or having avoidable conflict with several other team members. Though the "what" bore the fruit we all wanted to see, the "how" negated their overall performance, making them far less productive and effective than they may have thought they were. In such a case, if I find an employee excelling at the matrix we measure but doing a poor job in other areas such as maintaining harmony with other members of the team, I will have a conversation with them about it.

Specificity over Generalization

Being specific is the most important aspect of giving feedback. Don't tell someone in your team "People in the team say you've not been doing a good job," or "I've heard complaints about your performance from several members of the team". Generalities hardly ever help anyone, especially if you need to effect change through what you want to communicate. What is more helpful is giving them concrete examples such as," David informed me on Tuesday that for the past three weeks, you've submitted your work late, and it's negatively impacting his work" or "You are meeting all your weekly targets, but several of our vendors are complaining about your attitude. They said they sensed passive aggression and impatience when talking with you last week." You need to be able to provide concrete examples that your team members can learn from and course correct.

Make it Bi-directional

A healthy dynamic requires a bi-directional approach. If someone has feedback for you as the team leader, you never want them to sit on it. In my case, I want them to know that my door is open and that if they are frustrated with me, they can come in and sit down and talk about it.

All this communication must be prompt. Letting something fester does more damage in the long run. If something is left to fester, one day, the simplest thing can cause a blow-up, and all the effort you've put into developing your team can come crashing down like a house of cards. At that point, repairing the situation will require even more effort than if you had stayed on top of everything earlier on.

If you consider some of what we've shared, especially in Chapter 1, some of those qualities of a great leader, like trustworthiness and genuineness, should help make these bi-directional conversations and relationships easier and more natural for both parties to cultivate. With those qualities, you would have built trust and exercised active listening skills by this point in your team development efforts. I've noted, as perhaps you have, too, that when it comes to cultivating trust and opening up, people often don't care about your vocabulary, the letters after your name, or your acumen in your given field. What we all gravitate to, in regards to where we place our trust, is if we feel the efforts from the other party are coming from a genuine and authentic place of wanting us to do better. If the other party also wants better for themselves, these conversations are far easier.

Motivating Team Members

We all want to be fairly compensated for our contributions in any setting, especially in what we do for work. However, like most people, we all want to be acknowledged for the good we bring beyond the financial aspect. As a leader, your job is to ensure your team is adequately motivated to continue striving for excellence. This involves three aspects: letting your team members know they are heard, acknowledging their contribution, and showing them that they are valued. You acknowledge their contributions by recognizing their efforts and expressing gratitude for them on a one-to-one basis or in the presence of the group and third parties. Your team should not have any doubts as to whether they are valued or not.

Applying the Golden Rule

What can truly guide any leader in motivating team members is applying the golden rule. Consider how you feel when acknowledged and appreciated for efforts that would have otherwise gone unnoticed. Doesn't it feel great? Don't you feel more excited about giving more of yourself in that given context? We have to treat people the way we want to be treated ourselves.

As I already stated, a genuine "thank you" can be extremely impactful. We live in a world where, most of the time, efforts go unnoticed unless we are underperforming or causing problems for someone else. When someone consistently does a good or great job, it's easy for that to become "white noise" to us, and fail to give them that pat on the back now and then in acknowledgment of their continued consistency and effort.

Money Isn't Everything

Yes, this is work, and money is key to our concept of how we feel valued within this dynamic. However, money isn't the "Be all and End all". Of course, some of us are far more financially motivated than others, and it's important to be aware of which of your team members have that preference and how you can work that into whatever rewards you may wish to default to when you have the opportunity to give them more significant rewards and recognition.

Share the Positivity

I'm sure you've heard positive feedback about at least one member of your team at some point. As a leader, it feels great to hear good things about a team member you have.

It's especially pleasant when you have been strategic in getting them hired in the first place.

When you receive positive feedback about an individual on the team, make sure that you share that with them, preferably in a group setting. When you do, try to do it promptly and verbatim. We are all human beings, and the positive reinforcement that comes from such validation can be invigorating. All in all, an environment of positivity is encouraged.

Other than passing on the positivity within your team, depending on how high the stakes were, it may be a good idea to share your team member's success with your management. This helps your team members know that your concept of their value isn't just within the realm of your team's structure but also externally.

Making Motivational Moments

I mentioned "Motivational Moments" in Chapter 3: Developing your team. If you recall, "motivational moments" are these little nuggets of wisdom I would share with my team at every group meeting that we would have monthly. Oftentimes, I would present "Motivational Moments" on one slide in our group presentations. Typically, it would be a famous quote or meme relevant to what we collectively navigated as a team, organization, or even larger scale.

However, these were not the only occasions to motivate the team that I employed.

Incorporating "motivational moments" into your leadership repertoire as creatively as you can helps you set the tone for your team. It can also help your team persevere through the challenging times. To reinforce motivation, sometimes, I would go beyond sharing a quote and words of encouragement. Sometimes, I would give them tokens or symbols representing the message I felt they needed to internalize. In other cases, it would be taking the team or a team member out for lunch just as a simple thank you for the value they contributed to the team.

Pixie Dust

"I've been fortunate to have magical teams over the years in different companies. Sometimes though, people need to be reminded of just how awesome they are. In such an instance, during one of our monthly meetings, I knew the best way to achieve this was to get a little creative and give them a tangible symbol they could carry around with them wherever they went. I shared with them the following quote which I presented in Chapter 3:

"All You need is faith, trust and a little Pixie dust" -

Peter Pan[48]

Then I handed each member of my team a little vial of "pixie dust".

One member of my team had his pixie dust vial attached to his backpack. One day whilst he was with his daughter, he had an amusing conversation with her. She spotted the tiny container of sparkles and it captivated her that their daddy had that for himself! The little girl wanted to know where he got it from, and if she could have one of her own. His was in green and she wanted to know if they only came in green.

When he shared this story with me, I ordered one pink and one purple vial for her. Though this may sound rather whimsical or quirky. This story not only helped me establish a connection with this member of my team but also with his daughter. I know that neither his daughter nor him are likely to forget how this made them feel.

When I reflect on this experience and many others like it, I'm reminded of a quote attributed to Maya Angelou

---

[48] Barrie, J. M. *"All you need is Faith, Trust, and a little Pixie Dust"*

— *J.M. Barrie, Peter Pan*". Quotable Quotes. Quotes. GoodReads.com. https://www.goodreads.com/quotes/7440469-all-you-need-is-faith-trust-and-a-little-pixie

that highlights the importance of this type of approach: *"I've learned that people will forget what you said, people will forget what you did, but people will never forget how you made them feel.*[49]*"*

The financial cost of this was insignificant, yet, I managed to help create memories that will last a lifetime and maybe even encourage others to show up in surprising but positive ways. Later in this chapter, I share how we managed to integrate our team when our counterparts from Asia joined our workforce. Here's what one of my team members had to say about the motivation that she and her colleagues experienced as we became one united team:

"... I've never had a leader - before or after - quite like Tammy. When our team from Asia joined the US-based team, we didn't know quite what to expect. Fortunately, Tammy led us through a process that saw us becoming one multinationally functioning time thousands of miles apart.

One thing that she did when we were being integrated into the organization is she managed to convince

---

[49] GoodReads. "I've learned that people will forget what you said, people will forget what you did, but people will never forget how you made them feel. - Maya Angelou". Quotable Quotes.
(n.d.).https://www.goodreads.com/quotes/5934-i-ve-learned-that-people-will-forget-what-you-said-people

her bosses to mobilize resources for us to fly our team over to the US to engage and connect in person for the first time in our new working relationship with our US colleagues.

Tammy also had our whole team over to her home for Thanksgiving that year. This was a new experience for us, coming from a completely different culture. It was a privilege to be so warmly received and embraced. She and her daughters made a generous effort to cook Thanksgiving dinner for us and get to know us as individuals.

Apart from the opportunity to connect as a whole team, we also had the usual training exercises, as you would expect. We also had what we weren't sure we would expect: to be treated as equals to our US colleagues. I know that's because she knew that we were equals.

In some places, you get the sense that you're not looked at as others, but that was not the case with Tammy and the team she had already built. The same high expectations, the same high performance, and capabilities she believed our US colleagues had, she believed we had the same. And you know what? This belief in us made us strive for excellence. With someone investing so much in you, you don't want to disappoint them.

When we went back home, we knew who our new

leader and US colleagues were. We also knew that not only did the work we did matter, but we mattered as well. We knew this because of how exceptionally we were treated. To this day, Tammy remains a leader I admire but also now, a friend...."

- Lee

Avoiding Demotivational Moments

Being intentional about motivating your team is part of the equation, but so is being careful not to demotivate them. We've all been there: we receive crushing feedback that takes the wind right out of us. Maybe the critic was even completely right about what they were telling you about, but the way they told you made it far worse to receive. It's not uncommon for some people to shut down during such an encounter to protect themselves from the brunt of the emotional impact of the exchange.

Perhaps you've been in a position to receive constructive criticism in such a considerate manner that you managed to implement changes the other party recommended, and you came out successful at the end of it all. So, if you are going to be critical, make sure it is substantiated with facts and verifiable data. Additionally, don't forget to tailor your delivery of that criticism for effectiveness. If what you want to convey is purely subjective or based on opinion, it may demotivate your team members.

If a climate of demotivation is allowed to perpetuate, it accumulates and leads to a significant negative impact over time. This deterioration may look like lowered self-confidence of a given team member, a change in how they are showing up, an uncomfortable atmosphere in your office, and ultimately poor performance.

Managing Transformational Change

In Chapter 3: Developing Your Team, we touched upon aspects of change management within the "Stages of Team Development" that are helpful for your leadership journey, such as the change curve and driving acceptance of change. In maintaining high team performance, even within a mature and productive team, you will occasionally find yourself managing transformational change. In Chapter 1, we looked at an array of external and internal dynamics that impact your team as it functions in an organization. As change is a part of the flow of life, even in the workforce, we have to plan to manage it when it finds us.

Alignment Versus Agreement

You will face the need to align, agree, and sometimes do both. Ideally, we all want to work in organizations that we share values with. If you are lucky to be in one, that's great. However, even if you do enjoy this reality, there may come a time when you don't agree with a decision from management that impacts your team. When that happens, know that it's okay. You don't need to agree, but if you are to be successful at the job they pay you for, in those instances, you will need to be in alignment with their decisions. Let me share a personal experience with you:

Local to International

"Transformational change can be intensely tumultuous. Many years ago I had one such experience as I led a team at an organization that had decided to move from being a local organization to an international one.

All of a sudden, many of us had to start reporting to bosses who were not only new to us but in completely different countries. The upheaval was momentarily destabilizing. We didn't know how sweeping the changes would be and felt apprehensive about what would come next. As the title of a book by Mac Anderson goes, 'Change is Good, you go first.[50], in situations like this, sometimes we want to sit back and watch what happens next, afraid to

---

[50] Anderson, Mac. Feltenstein, Tom. "Change is Good...You Go First: 21 Ways to Inspire Change". Simple Truths. 2015, November 3.
https://www.amazon.com/Change-Good-You-Go-First/dp/149263042X#detailBullets_feature_div

make a move, in case it's the wrong one.

That situation made me step up and accept that though I didn't quite agree with the changes, we were in the throes of transformational change and it was my job to align with the change. My team's ability to adapt hinged strongly on my ability to do the same. It also meant ensuring that regardless of not agreeing with the changes, I did not show dissension and inadvertently created a mental paradigm in the minds of my team that would damage their ability to stay objective or even happy at this organization. The survival of my team, sustainability of my job, and a successful transition of the organization required this, of me and other leaders dealing with the same."

It's about recognizing what the change is, why it's happening, getting behind it, and helping your team get behind it, too, so you can succeed as an organization.

In some cases, you may find that not only do you not agree with the change or expectations thrust upon you in the workforce, but these changes do not align with your core values. When faced with such a situation that is unethical, deplorable, illegal, or simply against who you are as a person, alignment and agreement are not feasible options. In those instances, you must evaluate if exiting the organization may be your best course of action. We all need a line or boundaries that help us function successfully at an individual level. Here's another one of my personal examples:

24x7 Change Across Continents

"In a previous role, I led a team in the US and was given the responsibility of merging my team with another from a completely different country. Not only were the cultural differences, time zones, and other logistical matters new for everyone, we were faced with the challenge of how to make each individual team work as one.

I realized working as one was not enough. My two teams needed to 'become' one. If we were to offer round-the-clock service to our users, our working relationships needed to gel in such a seamless way that it looked as though we all worked in the same office space. Though each team was at the performing stage of team development, it was clear that our newly combined team was back at the first stage of team development - the forming stage.

This understanding was important because it helped me share with my new team a framework that helped make sense of everything. They knew to expect "Storming" next, and that some turbulence wasn't just normal but to be expected. During the stages of the team development cycle,

I was able to share with the team what needed to happen, who needed to be kept in the loop, and who the stakeholders were. An analysis of the stakeholders with them answering relevant questions about how the change impacts them helped us get a holistic view of the situation.

So, one of the efforts I made early on was to enlist input from members from both of the original teams. I needed them to have buy-in so that we all owned the result. It would not cut it if the result was considered 'Tammy's decision'. It needed to be collaborative so everyone knew they were a part of the decision-making process.

After a lot of effort, we managed to meld our team into one powerful and international team that was ultimately successful. Just as we saw the Stages of Team Development, I made a note of showing my team where we were at a given time and where we aimed to get to."

Stakeholder Analysis

Stakeholder analysis is a "...tool used to identify the project's stakeholders, issues they care about and how they will be impacted by the project"[51]. This tool will help you

---

[51] Hooroy, Leeron.Bottorff, Cassie. "What Is A Stakeholder Analysis? Everything You Need To Know". Business. 2022, August 7.
https://www.forbes.com/advisor/business/what-is-stakeholder-analysis/

understand who is involved in the success of your team and what they need to participate in or contribute as required.

Interviewing all the necessary stakeholders is part of conducting a stakeholder analysis. In those interviews, you aim to uncover each stakeholder's processes, needs, interests, and limitations.

As you re-organize your team, you need to ensure everyone's voice is heard. This includes the concerns and opinions of your team. It is important to temper your engagements for feedback with the understanding that though you want to hear what they have to say, it is still your job to ensure you make a decision, even if it is not the decision that they would like you to make. However, the commitment that I would encourage you to make and live by is a public resolve to consider their feedback. Active listening, a trait I highlighted as one key quality of great leaders, takes the forefront. Again, the simple but sincere acknowledgment of being heard can go a long way.

Planning for Continuity

You can get through a change, but if you don't sustain the change, all of your efforts are for naught. So, it all goes back to adjusting to transformational change in a sustainable way for you and your team. You need to ensure you reach the point that your team can sustain your operational model, and their new responsibilities and ways of doing things are thoroughly embedded in them. Again, you want to do such a great job that if and when you leave the organization, your team continues to be successful.

I liked to tell my previous teams that part of my job was to teach them how to do everything required whilst I was there, and their job was to continue it until they were informed by new leadership to take other measures. As you respond to transformational change, one of the questions you need to keep asking yourself and taking action in response to is: can these new measures be continued in the long term or even when I am gone? If not, what can I do to make this sustainable?

Driving a Healthy Narrative

With all the turmoil that transformational change may come with, having a healthy perspective as a leader is crucial. Make sure everyone in your team is clear on what's in it for them and how this change will impact them. Though positively framing the situation may seem disingenuous in certain scenarios, it's still your responsibility to present a narrative of the situation to your team that supports the efforts they need to take. This may look like saying, *"Team, this change is going to be uncomfortable, no doubt about it. Put your seat belts on, it's going to get bumpy but we will get through it together."*

Now, driving a healthy narrative isn't a once-off task. You need to maintain this stance throughout the change process. To accomplish that means maintaining those lines of communication and keeping them open for when your team and other stakeholders need an outlet. With a constant communication forum, you get to know what's going through the minds of everyone involved and what they are hearing about that you should know too. You have the opportunity to validate what they are feeling or experiencing. Rumors are inevitable in moments of transformational change. When you create these open communication forums, and people feel safe enough to share what they've been hearing, you can dispel any false narratives and ease the other party's fears and concerns.

Dealing with Stress

Stress is "a state of worry or mental tension caused by a difficult situation"[52]. Different studies over recent years have come to the same conclusion about stress: it is contagious. One study determined that our sweat carries hormones that inform others of our stress levels:

---

[52] The World Health Organization. "Stress". The World Health Organization. 2023, February 21. https://www.who.int/news-room/questions-and-answers/item/stress

"... New research shows that stress causes people to sweat special stress hormones, which are picked up by the olfactory senses of others. Your brain can even detect whether the "alarm pheromones" were released due to low stress or high stress...[53]"

It's not just our sweat that tells others how upset we are. Even watching someone over video or in person can pass on stress to the viewer without even directly communicating with one another:

".. A study from the Max Planck Institute for Cognitive and Brain Sciences and the Technische Universität Dresden found that even being around a stressed person, be it a loved one or a stranger, has the power to make someone stressed in a physically quantifiable way..."The fact that we could actually measure this empathic stress in the form of a significant hormone release was astonishing," said Veronika Engert, one of the study's authors....As expected, 95% of the people placed under direct stress showed signs of, well, stress. But 26% of observers had an increase in cortisol as well as a result of empathic stress. The impact of stress was

---

[53] Shawn, Achor. Gielan, Michelle. "Make Yourself Immune to Secondhand Stress". Stress Management. Harvard Business Review. 2015, September 2. https://hbr.org/2015/09/make-yourself-immune-to-secondhand-stress#:~:text=New%20research%20shows%20that%20stress,literally%20waft%20into%20your%20cubicle.

particularly high when a subject was observing a romantic partner in a stressful situation (40%) but it applied to strangers as well (10%).

When observers watched stressful events through a one-way mirror, 30% experienced a stressful response. Another 24% percent of observers were stressed when they watched the events unfold on video..." Time Magazine. 2014[54]

Similar studies prove that even just watching a stressed speaker can pass on stress to you[55].

Self-care

So, the question is: how do we overcome this? Over the years, I've deliberately tried to take care of myself and my team. I believe self-care - a topic that Chapter 7 is focused on will give us ample opportunity to dive deep into it. One aspect of self-care you need to encourage your team to participate in is taking their vacations, lunch breaks,

---

[54] Stampler, Laura. "Science Says Stress Is Contagious". Research. Health. Time Magazine. 2014, May 21. https://time.com/84080/stress-contagious/

[55] Dimitroff SJ, Kardan O, Necka EA, Decety J, Berman MG, Norman GJ. Physiological dynamics of stress contagion. Sci Rep. 2017 Jul 21;7(1):6168. doi: 10.1038/s41598-017-05811-1. PMID: 28733589; PMCID: PMC5522461. https://www.ncbi.nlm.nih.gov/pmc/articles/PMC5522461/

and designated time off.

This is an area that I know can be tricky to navigate. As a leader, we may encourage our team to take those holidays and not let work eat up the time they ought to spend resting and relaxing with their loved ones, but fail to optimally do the same. I truly believe this is a growth area that many of us leaders can work toward improving. We need to learn to leave our work at home when we are home and be present with those we love. Not only will our loved ones thank us, but we will see how nourishing switching off every day is to reset and come back to work with renewed energy the next day.

If a high-performing team member tells me they will need to come in 15 minutes or 30 minutes late several days a week because they need to pass by the gym each morning, I am happy to accommodate them. If their performance stays up, those gym sessions serve that team member and, in turn, the team.

Decompression Sessions

In a number of the roles I took, stress came with the territory. With that understanding, I realized having special blocks of time to "decompress" was crucial to my team's mental health. I talked about "decompression sessions" in previous chapters and how they were beneficial for helping our teams bond and ensuring we get some respite during the hustle and bustle that we were constantly exposed to or managing. Some would consider these sessions very out of the box, and I would agree. But if you can recall, creativity is one of the qualities of a great leader.

These sessions were typically fun bonding sessions, but also allowed team members to sit and vent with their colleagues. The opportunity to gain validation from a peer and its therapeutic benefits could not be understated.

My Message to You

I've heard it said that a sign of a great leader is that the team they build can survive without them. And I believe it. In the absence of a great leader, a team must not only survive but thrive. That is almost inevitable if you have instilled in each of them the core principles of being a high-performing team. Furthermore, I know that these core principles will serve each of your team members within their team or wherever their careers take them as they advance.

Having stated this multiple times, it's still worth repeating: all of this is hard work. For most of us, dealing with each other's humanity is challenging. It requires a significant investment of energy and team to get right. It means being deliberate and making space to accommodate this people-centered approach in business activities daily.

Having looked at how to sustain a high-performing team, we're switching our focus to performance management. How do you get the best out of your team? How do you guide a struggling performer toward excellence? How do you help a good performer become excellent at what they do? And how do you help an excellent performer stay consistent in how they show up in your team? We will look at all of this in the next chapter.

Chapter 6

Performance

"Measurement is the first step that leads to control and eventually to improvement. If you can't measure something, you can't understand it. If you can't understand it, you can't control it. If you can't control it, you can't improve it." — H. James Harrington[56]

In the previous chapter, we focused on how you and your team can maintain high performance. In this chapter, we will focus on the concept of performance and all the elements around it that you will need to lead and orchestrate, such as responses to your team's performance,

---

[56] GoodReads. "Measurement is the first step that leads to control and eventually to improvement. If you can't measure something, you can't understand it. If you can't understand it, you can't control it. If you can't control it, you can't improve it."— H. James Harrington". Quotable Quotes. (n.d.). https://www.goodreads.com/quotes/632992-measurement-is-the-first-step-that-leads-to-control-and

recognition, and rewards or consequences that you can deliver for all the different types of performance. We will begin by looking at the different types of performance (Excellent, Good, and Poor), and the different responses, recognition, and rewards each kind would attract. As there is a significant overlap between excellent and good performance, I've opted to present the various types of recognition and rewards in the Excellence section. Before concluding this chapter, we will discuss improvement opportunities that any team member has, regardless of their performance.

Before we go any further, let's take a moment to agree on what we mean by "performance" in this chapter. Here, we concentrate on "individual performance". *"Individual performance" being "the performance objectives specifically attributable to each (team member) reflective of his/her functional area and responsibilities, taking into consideration top Executive's evaluation of performance in that regard"*[57].

---

[57] Law Insider. "Individual Performance definition". Dictionary. (n.d.). https://www.lawinsider.com/dictionary/individual-performance#:~:text=Individual%20Performance%20means%20the%20performance,of%20performance%20in%20that%20regard.

Excellent Performance

The first of the three bands of performance (excellent, good, and poor) that we will look at is Excellent performance. Here, we will explore the ideal response you can take, and the types of recognition and rewards at your disposal to give your stars. I must note that the recognition and rewards I present here also apply to Good performance. To avoid repetition, I will only present them here but you must keep in mind that the same, though metered, is also relevant for good performance.

Response

Excellent performance is what we all want from ourselves and others. When we recognize excellent performance from our team, not only can we plan the most appropriate responses, rewards, and recognition for them, but also make efforts to help our team members maintain excellence.

In reality and perception, excellence must be considered adequately rewarded and recognized by your team members. No one wants to consistently do their best, only to notice their outstanding efforts are either ignored or inadequately responded to by those with the authority to impact their lives further positively. Ideally, the organization will have structures and protocols in place to address excellent performance. As a leader, it's your job to ensure that your champions get what they desire and are sufficiently motivated to maintain their performance. Recognition and rewards can help you accomplish this for anyone on your team who deserves it.

Recognition

When we talk of "Recognition", here we mean: *"... a company's acknowledgment of its staff for exceeding expectations. Companies recognize their employees to reinforce good behavior, performance or practices that result in positive effects and results for the business"*[58].

Recognition can be presented in different forms: written, oral, tangible, or any suitable combination of these. Tangible recognition could be a company trophy, "Employee of the Year" status, and similar examples.

Making sure you deliver that recognition most appropriately is also key. As with other factors mentioned in previous chapters: it's not just about the "what" (the substance), the "how" (the execution) is equally as vital. You wouldn't want to recognize excellent performance in a team

---

[58] Indeed Editorial Team. "Employee Recognition: Definition and Its Importance". 2023, February 4. https://www.indeed.com/career-advice/career-development/why-recognition-is-important

member but inadvertently plant or nourish the seeds of jealousy in other team members who attribute this recognition to favoritism or other unfair treatment. A well-thought-out approach can help you steer clear of any potential animosity whilst giving your champion-performers shine.

There are different levels of recognition that you may need to give. These levels are "one-on-one", "peer recognition" and "recognition beyond your team".

One on One

This type of recognition is the kind you offer to your team members directly and preferably in person, with the goal of the recipient of this information being only them. In this communication, you want to ensure your team member knows that you see their contribution, you acknowledge how much they are contributing, and you appreciate and value it.

Peer Recognition

Another type of recognition that you can give your team members when they perform excellently is peer recognition. This is the type of recognition you share about a good or great performer directed at the team member's colleagues. The goal with this type of recognition is to ensure that you are giving your team members the credit that's due to them in light of their admirable efforts. For this approach to be successful, you must apply balance, specificity, and genuineness, and sometimes even present how this performance benefits the team.

Balance is important because you don't want to come across as a leader who gives preferential treatment or attention to one of your team members over others. Coming across as someone who plays favorites only takes away from your credibility as an impartial and credible leader. Sometimes, you may have a team member who is consistently outstanding in their efforts. To attain balance and avoid the appearance of favoritism, you may need to meter your recognition and direct some of what you would have presented to them in a peer setting on a one-on-one basis instead. However, this does not mean you don't give them the peer recognition they deserve. You just need to ensure that whatever you present to the team is fact-based and indisputably substantiated against what the organization and team are trying to achieve.

When you are specific about what you are recognizing someone's performance for - in light of your team goals and objectives, you take away the plausibility of any type of favoritism at play. It also helps the team member whose performance you are applauding to not come off as an attention seeker or sycophant.

We can all mostly see or sense when statements or acts are disingenuous. This recognition presented in the presence of your celebrated team member must be completely genuine. You don't want to come off as fake or dishonest with any of your team because it takes away from any efforts you may have already made all along.

Here's an example of how you might present such praise about a star performer to your team. Let's call him Rupert:

"Rupert managed to accomplish his task on the ABC Project in 25% of the time that it would have taken earlier. This reduction in cycle time means our whole team can now expect to finish this whole project in two weeks instead of the projected three. "

By introducing how the star performer's productivity benefits the team at large, you help the rest of the team see this recognition from a camaraderie perspective instead of a competitive or combative one. By doing this, you help create a perspective that helps the team begin to rally behind your star.

Again, you may wish to offer a star performer more opportunities and resources because you know or believe they can utilize them best and accomplish excellent results with them. That is quite understandable but should be handled with the utmost care, again, to avoid the appearance of undesired preferential treatment. So, making it clear to the team why they are being offered or allocated these opportunities or resources that others may not have, in alignment with their ongoing excellence, can help justify and defuse any potential misunderstandings with your team.

Recognition Beyond the Team

This is the third type of recognition you can offer your high performers. All the types of recognition you can deliver to your performers have great benefits, but this type of recognition- beyond the team- can offer your star performer even more value. If I receive an email from a happy customer about one of my team members doing a wonderful job, it doesn't end with just one-on-one recognition and peer recognition. In the most appropriate cases, I take it to the top.

By taking this positive feedback about my team members to the appropriate upper leadership or management in the organization, upper leadership can see that there is external recognition of your team's output. It is also an opportunity to present validation for the praises you may have already given about this particular team member.

When that external recognition comes in, it's no longer a matter of your opinion or perspective as a leader. In this situation, what you are conveying isn't coming from you and backs up what you may have been saying all along.

Rewards

Sometimes, the distinction between recognition and rewards can get a little fuzzy. Some may consider recognition, in and of itself, a type of reward. That's because you would publicly say that a given person has done a fabulous job, regardless of the platform. To accommodate this train of thought, I present public recognition, alongside tokens of appreciation and financial rewards, as different types of rewards you can offer your team when appropriate.

Public Recognition

"Employee of the Month / Year" awards with their accompanying framed placards or photos are one way of publicly recognizing your stars. With some creativity, you may find other ways to present public recognition toward your team for different performance indicators they managed to meet or exceed.

Token of Appreciation

Though seemingly small and insignificant to others, tokens of appreciation may carry a lot of weight for the recipient and those witnessing the gesture. This gesture, indicating that efforts are not going unnoticed or that appreciation of these efforts is beyond a simple "thank you", can mean a lot to those receiving it.

It's also key that you stay attuned to your team's needs. Sometimes, leaders or organizations will offer tokens of appreciation of a value that the recipients would have preferred in monetary terms instead. Knowing what your team prefers in a given context may help you deliver tokens of appreciation - and rewards in general - that mean something to the people being granted them.

Financial Reward

At the very least, most employees appreciate financial incentives much beyond everything else you can offer. This is reasonable since most of us work for a living to earn an income beyond the opportunity to do work that gives us a sense of purpose and fulfillment. Some financial rewards you can give your team members when they produce the results your team and organization need include promotions, performance awards/bonuses, and merit increases.

Promotion

When there is upward room for career advancement

for your high performers, consistent excellent results should ideally attract a promotion. If an organization doesn't have room for upward mobility career-wise, you may need to consider offering a bonus or merit increase instead of a promotion.

However, when there is room to promote your most excellent team members, promotion is something you should naturally consider. In some cases, you may even wish to recommend star performers to other parts of the organization when you recognize that there are no career advancement opportunities for them within your own. That's a difficult decision to make since that means your team would lose the value that they directly contribute to your team. However, the fact that their efforts are rewarded adequately - albeit not in your team, through your influence is a considerate and empathetic way to take care of the people in your team who are doing their utmost best to deliver.

Performance Award / Bonus

In compensation plans for many organizations, performance awards or bonuses are given to employees who meet specified performance levels of certain elements. If there is no provision for this within your organization, perhaps you can advocate on your team's behalf so such provisions are incorporated. This can be a legitimate way to incentivize that extra level of performance from your team members: the bigger the bonuses they receive, the more exceptional their performance is.

Merit Increase

In many organizations, compensation plans are adjusted upward periodically after the team member consistently delivers specified merit-related considerations. In some cases, this may be on an annual basis.

Your organization's policies and protocols, your team norms, and your discretion as the leader are all factors that can help you decide what's best and fair in each case of offering rewards and recognition for a given team member.

Good Performance

We can all agree that though excellent performance is desirable and even the goal, it's not always what we get from our team or give to them as their leaders. A more realistic and still acceptable expectation from a high-performing team is good performance.

The recognition and rewards we discussed in the Excellent Performance section above can be delivered to good performers but with some adjustments to create a distinction between what your team gets when they perform excellently and what they receive when they perform well. Your team must be aware of whatever distinctions you factor into the recognition and rewards you deliver for good performance and alternatively for excellent performance because of the motivation that this distinction can offer your team towards even greater productivity and ultimately excellent performance.

Another distinction between how you treat good performance and excellent performance is in your response to either.

Response

Just as you acknowledge excellent performance from a team member and the whole team, you need to do the same regarding good performance. Your response should also include recognition or inquisition of what your team member wants and a presentation to your team member of any specific areas of improvement that you identify.

Acknowledgment of Solid Performance

Your team member did a great job? Good for you, yourself as the leader, and the team at large! Don't just glory in them meeting and sometimes exceeding expectations. Let them know that you are aware of how well they are doing.

Recognition of What the Employee Wants

If you want to encourage your team to do better, even as they do a good job, you must know what they want. Having such a conversation with them about their career aspirations, and goals for their immediate and long-term future, can show how your team and organization's offering aligns with them, and vice versa. You can then craft opportunities, recognition, and rewards that are worthwhile for them at a very personal level.

Imagine with me that you have a team member doing a good job. They tell you that their ultimate desire is to transition from marketing to advertising in a career that allows them more room to be creative. Armed with this information, as they continue to perform well, you can give them public recognition with the right people in the organization and externally that help them get seen. Your public recognition acts as a testimonial of their solid performance. This further adds to any social clout externally to the organization or internally that may help them move towards that role they expressed a desire for.

Specific Areas for improvement

Since we are all human, there are always areas where we could do better. Delivering a good performance means there is room to deliver an excellent performance. As such, another part of the response required of you regarding good performance from your team member is identifying which areas or aspects of their performance could do with improvement and communicating that to them for their attention and remediation.

Poor Performance

The last classification of performance, and the hardest one to lead a team member out of, is Poor Performance. Unlike Excellent and Good performance, we may agree that poor performance does not attract any positive recognition or rewards.

Addressing poor performance is unpleasant for both you and the underperforming team member. This may be because it should be a critical juncture or turning point for the team member to awaken to the impact that their performance is having on their career, your team, and maybe even the organization. As such, the response to poor performance is significantly different and involves communicating with the relevant team members, remediation, documentation, and consequences of continued poor performance. Let's take a look at each of these.

Response

Making sure there are no surprises is part of an impactful response to the poor performance of your team members. By this, I mean, your team members should not be in the dark regarding what you think about their performance until it is too late. Ideally, throughout the weeks, months, and years, they are made aware of any inadequacies of their performance that they have the power to address. The initial months of employment and the monthly one-to-one meetings are fitting occasions for you to carry out fact-based discussions with any underperforming employee. It is unfair to present their poor performance during their annual performance review at the end of the year without giving them your periodic assessment all along for them to address. That is, even if the argument is that their job description was enough for them to see that they were not doing good enough work.

They need to know that there are issues and be allowed to work on those issues. Your approach needs to be ongoing, timely, and consistent. If their performance significantly deviates from their expected performance, you need to ensure that you continue monitoring their performance and communicating with them any continued or consistent regression or even positive improvements.

Maintaining a consistent, ongoing, and timely approach benefits everyone for different reasons. Primarily this is important for your team because their improved performance positively impacts the team and organization. The sooner they right their ship, the sooner this positive impact starts to add value to the team. A benefit that the underperforming team member gets from this kind of approach - especially regarding timeliness- is that they can still get an opportunity to get rewarded or recognition if their changes are substantial or last long enough. Typically, merit increases and performance increases happen annually. If you find a team member is performing inadequately in February, for example, sharing your feedback on their performance immediately, may be a god-sent. If they are willing and can work hard, they may use the year's remaining months to turn their performance around and maybe even get a merit or a performance increase.

Typically, I would begin a response to poor performance with an in-person conversation with the underperforming team member, where possible. I would sit with them and lay out the situation with them, supported by verifiable data and metrics about their performance concerning team and organization expectations. As stated, this is an uncomfortable process, and the best thing you can do is be direct when you start this conversation. Beating about the bush will not help. Let the other party know, right off the bat, that the conversation you've invited them to will likely not be pleasant and that your goal is to share with them the aspects of their role that aren't going well to have them work towards fixing them.

Keeping a personal and empathetic stance on this process is also still necessary. This in-person conversation should be on a one-to-one basis and not in the presence of others, where the individual might feel attacked, defensive, or even targeted.

As a result of the ongoing one-to-one meetings and accountability meetings that my team-building process requires, your established relationships with your team will allow them to tell you when another colleague is performing poorly. If poor performance of a team member is brought to your attention by their colleagues or someone else in or outside of the organization, you may need to prepare adequate responses for them, too. If those bringing the situation to your attention are the team member's colleagues, you have the added challenge of ensuring that your response not only makes them feel heard, with intentions of actually handling the situation, but also remaining empathetic and respectful towards the underperforming employee in their absence. A simple acknowledgment of "I understand" is all you need to give to that person so that they know that you've heard them and are taking care of it.

Remediation

Responding appropriately to a team member's performance is the first part of addressing poor performance. The next and equally important part of this job is remediation. You need to share with the underperforming team members how they can fix the issues you have addressed. They need to make the necessary efforts to rectify those issues. Effective remediation should lead to improved performance.

Remediation will require you to develop and issue the team member a customized Performance Improvement Plan (PIP) with review meetings at periodic intervals where you assess any agreed-upon measurable outcomes. I mentioned this plan in earlier chapters. A PIP is *"... a document that aims to help employees who are not meeting job performance goals. A PIP covers specific areas of performance deficiencies, identifies skills or training gaps, and sets clear expectations for an associate's future conduct. Objectives must be met within a certain period, and failure to do so may result in employment actions (such as termination)...*"[59].

In most cases, you will work with the Personnel department on some of the employment or contractual-related aspects of taking this path. The Personnel department will provide you with additional support in key aspects of implementation of this plan, such as determining whether or not a PIP is necessary and also its duration.

Consequences

Though termination of the team member's contract is the most severe consequence that ongoing poor performance would attract, depending on the severity of the situation, there are other less drastic and more fitting measures that you can take.

When it comes to bonuses, you may inform the underperforming member that this may mean they will get a lower amount for their annual bonus. Another potential consequence you can make your team members aware of is the impact that their performance may have on their annual merit increase. If applicable, this may mean informing them

---

[59] Gartner. "Performance Improvement Plan (PIP)". Gartner Glossary. (n.d.). https://www.gartner.com/en/human-resources/glossary/performance-improvement-plan-pip-#:~:text=A%20performance%20improvement%20plan%20(PIP,for%20an%20associate's%20future%20conduct.

that they will not receive any merit increase that year, again depending on their performance and efforts in rectifying it.

You may have an instance where a poorly performing team member disagrees with your performance assessment. This becomes a very interesting conversation and quite tricky to navigate if you do not adequately document their performance over their tenure. I've had this happen before, and I've found that the best way to handle this is through open and honest dialogue with them, again substantiated by facts. In a one-to-one setting, I ask them to share why they feel their performance differs from my assessment. To agree, you need to first understand their perspective, only then does it make sense to present the facts and data validating your own.

If your evaluation of their performance is backed up by reports from this individual's colleagues, this is the time to give this individual detailed information of specific experiences where their performance fell short and negatively impacted their colleague's efforts in the team.

At times, colleagues may give you information about another's poor performance with the request that they remain nameless. You must remain informative and tactful as you respect the confidentiality request other team members requested.

When you come to a scenario where you and the other party differ in perspectives - even though your assessment is based on hard facts, you may find that it truly boils down to an issue of self-awareness. Without self-awareness, it can be hard to note how we are doing or impacting others, even regarding performance. Inviting people to reflect on their efforts can help them awaken to the divide between how well they thought they were doing and how they were doing. Here's one particular example that stands out for me where I experienced this scenario firsthand and how I handled it:

A Different World

"We all make career changes. I entered the work world with a background in Education before I became an expert in the CyberSecurity space. I often feel people with diverse backgrounds have brand new perspectives to offer those who have only known one world. One individual that I recall came from a law enforcement background. "In the field"-type of law enforcement work is massively different from a typical corporate America setting. Sadly, this lady brought a certain level of aggression from your previous career into our team.

Though we can all appreciate the relevance and importance of such careers, some of the lingo, mannerisms, and attitudes that come with it, may be inappropriate and unpalatable for the office setting. The underlying disdain that employees had with how she carried herself was that she appeared to be putting herself on a pedestal. It seemed she had not reconciled with the reality that she was no longer downtown, locking up bad guys. Though I was her leader, I think the verbiage of "Commander" or "Sergeant" was not terminology that worked for the type of team that I built and nurtured. Other people coming from a law enforcement background who worked in the organization found her demeanor and incessant use of such terminology infuriating.

Even more important than the friction she encountered with other members of the team, this employee in question did not perform as well as she believed. When I brought this to her attention, she did not agree with my assessment, which I presented with verifiable facts and reports from others that had been negatively impacted by her level of performance.

So, when she was finally put on a Performance Improvement Plan, she was not happy. She disagreed with my assessment of her performance and was emphatic about how well she was doing. Eventually, while implementing her PIP, she decided that the organization was not the best fit for her, and she resigned."

I wouldn't want to end this section on a low note. Let me share with you a more heartwarming experience I had with another employee whose success is one of my joys to recall to this day:

Rising Through the Ranks

"Henz started his work life as a short-order cook. When he joined the corporate world, he began his career there in the mailroom. Henz was likable, ambitious, and hardworking. You could see that he put in every opportunity he got.

Gradually he worked his way up in the organization and eventually qualified and applied for an opportunity in a team that I led. He succeeded in the interviews and became one of my team members.

Unfortunately, over some time I noticed that his performance was not up to par. I had a lot of faith in his abilities and truly hoped he would do well. Eventually, we reached the point where his performance was still unsatisfactory and I had to put him on a PIP.

I was not surprised that he was unhappy about being put on this structured program. However, what surprised me was how he disagreed with my assessment of his performance. Fortunately, he came to understand my perspective when I walked him through the data and reports that had come through from several members of the team. One key concern that had come up was how he would sometimes be unavailable during the work day. Instead of leaving his desk at the end of the day as expected, he would leave at around 2 pm. This was likely a remnant of his former career where there was that type of flexibility. Unfortunately, his new role - in this corporate setting, did not allow for that.

Henz really stepped up to the challenge and became one of my most inspiring team members. He invested in learning and applying new skills, and in relating better with his teammates.

I am pleased to say that to date, he has advanced from the level he was at when I was his leader to a more technical and more rewarding role within the same company. I think this boils down to his eventual willingness to accept that he had room for improvement and working towards that improvement."

Lastly, let's not forget the positive consequences that improved performance will attract. Ensure that it is also clear to the employee that you've addressed their current poor performance.

Documentation

Other than an appropriate response, remediation, and suitable consequences, you need to document the whole process. The performance of the underperforming individual may become the cause for termination. The Personnel Department will need proper documentation to fulfill their end of the organization's employment contract and avoid any potential labor law infringements and other such potential reasons for lawsuits.

When you have sufficient documentation, you can present this to the employee in question and to the Personnel Department as evidence of your attempts to address the issues that were ultimately not adequately resolved despite your efforts. This documentation should include dates, subjects of these meetings, the content of discussions, and agreed-upon resolutions. In this documentation, you would make sure that what was done and what wasn't done is included. You would, therefore, indicate that despite your efforts, you could not turn this individual's performance around.

Improvement Opportunities

I've mentioned it before: no matter how good you

are, there is always room for improvement. Excellent performers and Good performers will have improvement opportunities offered to them. When conducting performance reviews for each of your team members, you can rate or grade them on different aspects, typically based on whether they meet expectations, exceed expectations, or do not meet expectations.

When you assess your findings, you should note any areas marked with "Does not meet expectations". A compiled list of these forms a good basis for the improvement opportunities that would be most beneficial and necessary for that specific individual.

Of course, when an employee presents a solid performance, you must begin with acknowledging the specifics of that solid performance before you begin to talk about improvement opportunities. This recount of their solid performance would stem from the aspects of their performance review where they "met expectations".

Regarding improvement opportunities, talk to your team members about where they are in their performance, understand what they enjoy, and whether or not they are happy doing what they are currently doing. During this exercise of presenting improvement opportunities, you have to look at how they are accomplishing what they are accomplishing and how they are accomplishing it. Again, there are nuances and layers to a good performance. Being technically brilliant, for example, doesn't excuse them from treating other members of a team poorly. When someone shows up this way, I share with them that their "how" (interpersonal relationship skills) needs immediate improvement, such as training. If a team member does a great job but seems to struggle with time management, I would ensure they become aware of this concern and assist them in finding a fitting time-management training, online program, or coaching to help them overcome this difficulty.

My Message to You

Assessing performance is at the heart of steering a high-performing team. Conveying the individual performance of a team member, due to the significant positive and negative impact that it can have on them as individuals or as a team, makes much of the dialogue about individual performance often personally impactful for whomever you are assessing.

When handling poor performance, the conversation becomes even more sensitive and must be handled with the utmost delicacy and all relevant protocols of your organization. If you think back to the story I presented to you about Henz, a former team member of mine, hopefully, you can see that even individuals who are performing poorly today can be guided toward excellence. However, it requires you to give them the guidance, support, respect, and sensitivity the matter requires. If approached in the right manner, even these unpleasant experiences where you have to present the facts to a poorly performing individual can become moments that transform their lives and move them towards a whole new beginning.

You must take time to craft and prepare your responses, especially those for poor performance. Ahead of time, you need to internalize and be ready to share the main message of your response with the individual and what you would want them to take away from it. This key aspect of personnel development warrants proper preparation, planning, time, and execution.

Lastly, it is worth remembering the importance of grace during these efforts. The same treatment that you would desire for yourself in their shoes is what you should aim to deliver every time you evaluate and respond to the different types of performance and potential areas of improvement that any member of your team may have. Keep in mind how every opportunity - even the seemingly hard ones, may carry with it moments that can imprint on your team member's life for the rest of their lives. Let this remind you of what an honor and responsibility your leadership role is to build and not demolish those you influence.

As we conclude this topic on the performance of your team, we will now move on to the last chapter of my book. Most of what we discussed was team-facing. In this last chapter, we will take a moment to raise a mirror and look at you - the leader. I will also share my personal experiences, many of which I imagine you may have dealt with or will one day deal with, too. A number of these issues may appear out of place within a book about team building, transformational leadership, and creating sustainable teams, but I'll tell you something I learned about leadership that validates why this next chapter is important: if you aren't taking care of yourself and staying on top of what affects you personally,

Chapter 7

Self-Care

Don't Forget To Take Care of You

"Rest and self-care are so important. When you take time to replenish your spirit, it allows you to serve others from the overflow. You cannot serve from an empty vessel." — Eleanor Brownn[60]

Every single one of us is a multifaceted individual. If you look at whatever or whoever you are responsible to or for, the list may be long and sometimes overwhelming. Work, family, social circles, religious and political affiliations,

---

[60] GoodReads. *"Rest and self-care are so important. When you take time to replenish your spirit, it allows you to serve others from the overflow. You cannot serve from an empty vessel."*

— *Eleanor Brownn".* Quotable Quotes. (n.d.).https://www.goodreads.com/quotes/4295989-rest-and-self-care-are-so-important-when-you-take-time

and aspirations all require some level of commitment. In the mix of it all, life events call for you to make some adjustments to accommodate emergencies and other life-impacting events.

As I have stated before, we are not just leaders. We do not operate in vacuums. A bad day at home can lead to a challenging day at work and vice versa. These other aspects of our lives impact us in terms of how effective we are in the workforce and overall, in general. If we want to give ourselves the best chance for overall success, we need to make sure caring for ourselves is part of our strategy for our leadership success.

I shared quite a bit about myself in the Preface of this book. You may have noted that I have experienced what some would consider extreme adversity. I agree. I have had financial setbacks, scraped my way out of debt, been the main caregiver to multiple loved ones facing devastating diagnoses, overcame a divorce, and raised two strong daughters alone as a single mom working full time in corporate America whilst still trying to contribute towards mentorship, coaching promising individuals with potential, and organizations I care about like the Girl Scouts and industry associations.

With all these demands and challenges, somehow, I

have been fortunate enough to cultivate a successful career as a leader spanning decades. How is this possible? I think part of it boils down to the different facets of self-care that I prioritize. Neglecting these would not only degrade the quality of my life but also decrease my effectiveness in my roles at work.

So, what I will share with you in this chapter is everything that makes it possible for me to do everything else in this book. This superglue holds the rest of this together, helping me consistently succeed at work through the most unimaginable curveballs life has thrown at me. To do this chapter justice, I will have to get a bit more personal than in previous chapters. As you read it, I invite you to reflect on your life and particular circumstances. Maybe what's worked for me will not be an exact fit for you, but I hope, at the very least, it gets you thinking about what you can do to take better care of yourself and optimize yourself for overall leadership success. As my therapist used to remind me, *"In an airplane, they repeat - put your oxygen mask on first before you help others".* Here, we learn how to do that before we need to.

We will look at Establishing healthy boundaries, Work-Life Balance, Mental & Emotional Self-Care, and Physical Self-Care.

Knowing Your Boundaries

Boundaries, "unofficial rules about what should not be done: limits that define acceptable behavior" are an integral part of self-care[61]. Since we are all different, we should accept that our boundaries may vary. What may be unacceptable to you may be acceptable to me. And the opposite may also be true. Your story and life outside of the office will likely influence and shape your work life.

Sometimes, we may not know our boundaries until we experience someone, something, or even ourselves violating them. It's necessary to take time to understand ourselves and what we find acceptable behavior from others in our work settings and ensure we communicate effectively so that we help establish and maintain harmony inside ourselves and externally. We may not always get it right, but the goal should be that we aim for and default to whatever gives us that harmony. Here's a personal story with my context:

Single-Working Mom Diaries

"Our boundaries define our personal space – and we need to be sovereign there in order to be able to step into

---

[61] https://www.britannica.com/dictionary/boundary

our full power and potential." - Jessica Moore[62]

I am a single mom with two amazing daughters.. Over the years, as I raised my two daughters, one thing remained paramount: my girls were my top priority. My mother was diagnosed with cancer three different times and is now a cancer survivor of more than 25 years. She also became my top priority as I became her primary caregiver. As a result of my responsibilities to my family, I set some firm boundaries to ensure their well-being and care.

However, if my daughters or mother needed me - especially in the case of emergencies, I needed to be able to get to them as soon as possible, preferably in under 10-15 minutes. This meant I typically looked for and accepted work opportunities that were within that parameter to drive to.

Though I have always had demanding jobs, I understood and recognized what I was willing to give up and what I wasn't as a result of my career aspirations. For example, I could not travel every week or month. I consciously decided to travel only occasionally.

---

[62] Barkley, Sarah. "17 Inspiring Quotes About Setting Healthy Boundaries". Health. 2023, May 3. https://psychcentral.com/health/quotes-healthy-boundaries#the-need-for-boundaries

In one instance, I passed on taking up a leadership training program because I knew how it would not work with the level of presence I desired to give my children. Taking up this program would have meant not being able to get my girls on and off the bus. It also meant I wouldn't be able to attend their school events as much as I would normally do. For me, that was unimaginable. I did not want to put myself in a situation where work denied me the opportunity to show up for my girls as much as I felt necessary. Turning down that opportunity made sure that I would not have to tackle that situation.

Now that my children are older, I've adjusted some of my considerations that affect which jobs I take up, including how far they are. I no longer limit my search to jobs that are within a short drive, I am open to finding work even an hour away. This is because I know my children don't need me as much and because I have support in caring for my mother which gives me the room to comfortably make these adjustments.

As a result of these personal desires, when it came to selecting companies to work for, I paid a great deal of attention to the company culture. Did it mesh well with my family-centered approach to life or was it a stoic enterprise that focused solely on the bottom line? Knowing this in advance, and choosing the best fit helped me have an easier go at maintaining my boundaries, caring for my loved ones, and honoring my most authentic self.

If you recall from Chapter 1, I shared with you some qualities a great leader has. One of them was "Self-reflection" - looking inward. That ability to assess yourself and exercise self-awareness - know who you are and what makes you tick - is crucial in setting healthy boundaries and taking great care of yourself. It will allow you to know your limits, where you have some wiggle room for compromise, what company culture is compatible with your values, what sacrifices you are willing to make for your interests, and when need be, the organization you choose to work for.

You are allowed to adjust your boundaries as you see fit because life changes. Sometimes, life demands that we make these changes. Consider what happened to all of us during the global COVID-19 pandemic. Adjusting our boundaries to accommodate those changes, instead of remaining rigid, was not only part of sustained progress and growth but also part of being more effective at whatever we did.

Work-Life Balance

Sometimes, you find yourself fortunate enough to

work in an organization that values a "work-life" balance. I've been lucky enough to experience the comfort and seamlessness that come with shared values at a corporate level with my own. One of the companies I worked for was an early adopter of the whole concept. I worked for them before working from home or remotely was even an option, and yet their flexibility allowed me and other employees to operate in such a manner. They trusted that we would still be productive and get the job done. Back then, it meant having the flexibility to work even just one day a week from home. In those days, even that was huge because very few other companies even thought of the concept, let alone allowed it.

As with knowing your boundaries and setting them, establishing a work-life balance depends on how well you know yourself. Only then can you make supportive, disciplined, and productivity-oriented decisions. It doesn't help you if you know that you simply can't work at home because you feel powerless against all the distractions you find yourself surrounded by.

For some of us, work-from-home simply can't be an option, and we need to determine that for ourselves. Let's not forget that your ability to create balance may need some help. This may need sitting down with an advisor, coach, mentor, friend, therapist, or counselor and approaching this from whatever angle works for you. You may even find that your distractibility is not all about discipline through some professional assistance.

Some of us know that even though we are working from home, we can throw a load of laundry into the wash, make a quick lunch, and still get all our day's work done without breaking a sweat. If we were in the office, we probably would have taken a lunch break and spent a couple of minutes in the hallway, sipping coffee for 15 minutes and chatting with our co-workers anyway, and the time expense could make no difference with our at-home non-work related activities. It boils down to how diligent you can get yourself to behave. Of course, sometimes, it isn't about your ability to exercise diligence but the needs of your loved ones that require you to take a more concentrated approach to your work-life matters.

How Did You Know It Was Okay?

"As a single mom, you just have to realize that the day-to-day is going to be a ****show, for lack of a better phrase. You have to be flexible, be there for school drop offs, pick ups, and the madness of it all." - Christine Michel Carter[63]

---

[63] https://www.countryliving.com/life/entertainment/g19736231/single-mom-

"Tammy and I used to work at the same company. That's how we became friends, and we are still close friends over twenty years later. I remember when her daughters were very young. She was a single mom and you could tell how dedicated to our kids she was. She tried to make every Parent Teacher Conference. If either of her daughters had an end-of-week performance, or needed to go to camp in the summer, she made it happen or at least tried her best. At the same time, she had to ensure her mom got the treatment and support she needed. All this whilst trying to rise the corporate ladder.

You see, I was fortunate to have my husband to help me raise our child. I put in a lot of work and sacrifices that allowed me to lead large teams successfully over a decade. If I couldn't do something important for our child my husband would or we would figure something out together. As a team, we were able to make it work, and even then sometimes it could still be tricky.

There were times Tammy would put up a notice on her door, notifying the office of the hours she would be out and when she would be next available. This was novel, in fact, almost unheard of at the time. Typically, you were at work, unless you called in sick or on leave.

quotes/?slide=2

As I reflected on all this, I asked Tammy, "How did you know that it was okay?"

She simply responded, "I didn't have a choice."

- Naomi

Then, of course, there is love. Whatever your marital status, if you have a demanding job, your job may have an impact on your marriage or union. If you are searching for love, I would advise you to make it clear to your potential partner how your career may impact how you show up in the relationship. Those reports you take home to finish, that late-night email you need to respond to, or a phone call you feel compelled to respond to during dinner time. These are all scenarios that someone interested in building a life with you would have to expect to encounter on occasion. If you choose, you could try to figure out boundaries that help you find the right balance.

As you advance in your career, it may come with influence, growing financial capacity, and even power. If you're a single woman, these beneficial things may seem intimidating to some potential suitors. You must find a partner who is - if not fully embracing your success and its benefits, at least willing to work with it all as part of what being with you comes with. If your partner is not intimidated by your financial capacity and potential but instead supports you, then you have a good thing going.

I've noticed something peculiar from myself and many of my friends who've spent a large part of their lives independently. The matter of peculiarity is how hard it is to kick back and let someone else do what you've done for yourself all along. Paying attention to your behavior and how you impact others can help you see where you can give people more room to participate proactively. There are not many parts of this book where I advise you to "not do as I do but do as I say," but this is one of those rare instances. I encourage you to lean back more in your relationships and allow yourself to be more of a partner and less of a leader.

As I conclude this section on Work-Life Balance, I think it would be a great time to share different perspectives of how I approached this aspect over the years. Samantha and Erin, my daughters, were interviewed to share their experiences growing up. Here's what they had to say:

Daughters of a Working Single-Mom"...a single parent, an honest-to-God buck-stops-with-me single parent was a rare species." — C J Cooke

"... Mom just started her new job days ago. Last night she got home from work and took Gram to bingo.

Gram can play bingo at her assisted living home but Gram prefers bingo at the American Legion and mom likes to make sure she takes her there.

Over the past months that mom was changing jobs, she devoted her time to Gram. She was able to do that because nothing from work would come up like a work dinner or something.

I've seen my mom show up for Gram for simple things like this and even for emergencies like when Gram fell, hit her head, was bleeding, and needed to go to the hospital. In instances like those, even though she was working, she would drop everything to ensure that she was there so Gram got the care she needed.

In instances where mom couldn't be there, either I, my older sister - Samantha, or one of mom's friends would be there to help balance things out. So, we all try to the best we all can..."

- Erin (my youngest daughter)

As a young leader, I would like you not to repeat any mistakes I made along the way. For that reason, I asked my daughters a question that may help you balance your work-life better than me: *"Growing up, what could I have done better?"*

Here's part of what my oldest - Samantha, had to say:

"... Because she was a single mom, she couldn't go out and do all the other things she wanted to do all the time. When she did go out, with her friends, she would make sure that we were taken care of first.

Growing up, my sister and I couldn't understand how much mom had to adjust her life for us. She would leave work early on some days so that she could take us to the doctor or something else that had to do with us. She would lead Girl Scouts when she could and show up at our Saturday softball games more often than not. She's working much further from home now that we are both adults. Back then though, she made sure it was just a matter of minutes to get to us in case something major happened. I currently live in a different State and Erin is pretty independent but currently still at home with mom. Mom understands that we can handle most things ourselves but when we can't, we know she'll always be there to help us through it.

When both Erin and I look back, we know mom did a great job raising us and we can't think of much that we would have had her do differently. Looking back, one thing that both Erin and I agree on is maybe she could have tried to "leave work at work" more. Those nights when I'd rather relax on the couch, maybe watching a show together but *though mom was there, she had to work on her PC. Those felt like missed moments for camaraderie or bonding.*

In one of Mom's earlier jobs, she had to travel far more than the others that came after. On one occasion, Mom traveled to Malaysia for two weeks and boy did that period drag on! At that point, my sister wasn't yet comfortable with staying with other people or anywhere else, for that matter. As her older sister, I understood that Mom needed to go on that trip for work but I still found it hard to help Erin. Now that Erin's older, she thinks it may have been attachment anxiety that caused her all that discomfort back then..."

If you have children or dependents or have plans (or expectations) to have them in the future, I encourage you to pause and reflect on how you plan to navigate similar situations to what my children shared above. Now, let's talk about the next important way you can take care of yourself: physical care.

Physical Care

Physical care -particularly exercise - is extremely important, but it is one area that I am not excelling in at the moment. However, 2016 comes to mind when I consider myself to be at my best: physically and all around.

Looking fit is one thing, but being physically healthy is another. When discussing this topic, I'm leaning more on physical health than aesthetics. Though my daughters barely just entered adulthood, I want to make sure I am healthy to meet my future grandchildren and play with them without struggling.

As someone who has never been skinny because it isn't in my genetic makeup, I have still had times when my weight was at what I preferred, my body felt good, and I loved what I saw in the mirror. I remember climbing out of bed without hesitation and going for a walk each morning. I was also getting myself in bed earlier and enjoying quality sleep. However, I had undertaken an intensely restrictive diet, limiting my daily calories to 500, which helped make me drop significant weight. But the reality is that a maximum of 500 calories a day is not only highly restrictive but also unhealthy in the long term.

You may be doing much better in this area than I am. I know that if I am to return to enjoying the health benefits I experienced, I need a more sustainable, less restrictive way of getting there. We all do.

Mental & Emotional Care

Sometimes, what we need for optimal mental and

emotional wellbeing may be minor. Other times, we must invest more to secure our holistic well-being. Different situations warrant different types of approaches to manage your mental and emotional health. Let's look at this in three different contexts I like to call: small, big, and work.

Small Stuff

Attending to our mental and emotional care in minor ways may look like making a self-check when you feel yourself losing yourself. As a matter of transparency, let me share one instance I'm not particularly proud of:

Fast and Furious Food Incident When angry, count to ten before you speak. If very angry, count to one hundred.

- Thomas Jefferson[64]

"I don't usually lose my cool but when I do, it can be pretty intense. I cringe to think of one particular incident that illustrates this quite well. I had gotten home from a tough day at work and I was having car problems, which I had noted for some time. I needed to drop my car off one night for service. My two daughters were with me that night and it made sense to just grab some fast food for dinner whilst

---

[64] Brainy Quotes. "Anger Quotes". (n.d.).
https://www.brainyquote.com/quotes/thomas_jefferson_132201?src=t_anger

we were still finishing our errands.

We would order and eat and move on to the next thing on our to-do list. That's what I expected. But no. One of my daughters wanted to order from Kentucky Fried Chicken, and my other daughter wanted something from Burger King.

At the same time, I was trying to get a hold of a loved one who was supposed to pick us up after we dropped off the car for service. I called multiple times and they didn't answer. This annoyed me. Everything annoyed me.

I looked at my daughters and asked, "Are you serious that we just cannot get food at one place?"

I was frustrated that we couldn't all just order and make this day a little easier for me. I was angry with myself because I had led my daughters to believe that I would do whatever they wanted. I was annoyed that I couldn't secure our ride back home, and furious that simple tasks like these weren't easier to complete.

At some point, as I sped us off in a rage, I eventually gathered myself. I was able to ask myself: What the heck are you doing, Tammy? Why are you acting like this? What is going on in your brain right now?

These self-checks helped me pause, "breathe", and recalibrate. We got through this experience but it wasn't pleasant."

This silly experience is one most of us are familiar with: it's not the one annoying or bad thing that happened to you. It's the accumulation effect of all the annoyances, challenges, inconveniences, and slights that pile up and overwhelm you. In those moments, taking a moment to pause, breathe, and reflect on what you're doing can help you salvage an undesirable situation.

Big Stuff

If you recall what I shared with you in the Preface, I've experienced a lot of challenges. Multiple times in my life, I've relied on experts, in some cases, therapists, to help me overcome those challenges. Often, I've worked hard at being strong at work whilst accepting that I need help in other aspects of my life. If you find yourself in such predicaments, I hope you know it is okay. Knowing you need help and getting that help are fundamental to a lifestyle that includes healthy self-care. The help you may need may be therapy or professional health of other sorts. Sometimes, you need help taking care of your children or dependents. If you are strong or consider yourself strong, getting help may feel like a failure. I assure you, there is neither shame nor weakness in asking for or accepting help. Asking for help is one of the strongest displays of strength you can make. Mental health can not or should not be sidelined. None of us can afford that.

I would like to share with you a very sensitive story. As it is about losing a loved one from suicide, please feel free to skip it if you feel it may be best for you.

Tomorrow Will Be Better "No matter what happens, or how bad it seems today, life does go on, and it will be better tomorrow."

— Maya Angelou[65]

Imagine finding someone, seeing the universe in their eyes, and hoping to one day spend forever with them. You may be familiar with that experience of falling in love and all the hope and joy that comes with it. This time forever didn't come. This man that I loved so deeply one day, took his own life.

I wish he hadn't. I wish he had talked to me and told me what was hurting. By now, you should know that if he

---

[65] Good Reads. "No matter what happens, or how bad it seems today, life does go on, and it will be better tomorrow." — Maya Angelou". Quotable Quotes. (n.d.). https://www.goodreads.com/quotes/275019-no-matter-what-happens-or-how-bad-it-seems-today

had, I would have moved heaven and earth to make whatever pain he had gone away.

The pain of losing him, so suddenly and in such a way is a pain can't fully describe. After the shock died down, and I could start seeing through the fog of grief, anger, denial, and sadness, the reality that I couldn't fix it slowly set in. I couldn't change the outcome. That was hard to accept, especially when I'm so used to being proactive and taking the lead in emergencies. Eventually, my mind accepted the only sliver of hope it could: going forward, I would take extra care to see the signs and have the hard conversations we shy away from having because denying a situation feels easier than confronting it.

Since then, I've had this difficult conversation with many people I care about, conversations I probably would never have ventured to have, if it wasn't for this tragic loss I sometimes still can not believe happened.

I like to think that, even if my concerns were ill-placed, they still went away knowing that someone cared and valued their well-being."

This devastating experience made me ask: What can I learn from this situation, and what can I do going forward? That's what led me to the conversations I now have with people when I am concerned about their mental and emotional health. I ask two questions: "Do you feel like you are going to hurt yourself?". Secondly, "Do you feel like you want to hurt somebody else?"

These two questions will often cause the individual to pause before answering. After their feedback, I can guide them to get the help they need.

Work Stuff

Your workplace may provide you with support for your mental and emotional health. If that is an option for you, it is worth considering using this service as much as you need. If confidentiality issues between the therapist or counselor are concerns of yours, learning whether or not what you share is protected for only you two or if this is shared with your employers is a step you can take. In some organizations, what you share could end up in a report and impact your overall performance. Know what you are getting into before you do.

I have been fortunate enough to work at a few establishments with excellent mental and emotional health support. The professionals I sat with and received support from were invaluable in helping me stay productive at work and emotionally and mentally healthy everywhere.

If the possibility of your private conversations being shared bothers you, regardless of what policies are put in place to protect your privacy, that is a valid concern. Consider finding your own professional outside of the organization. If you have the resources, I encourage you to go for it and accept the expenses as an investment in your wellbeing, because your wellbeing is worth investing in.

When you find a service provider or professional that has done a great job with you, don't forget to recommend them when you find someone struggling with the same challenges you did. You never know the impact that they may have and how deeply that person needs the help.

My Message to You

Exercising self-care shouldn't be something we do when breaking down and at the end of our rope. These efforts can serve us best when woven into the very fabric of our lives. Sometimes, the changes in our lives will require us to do more or else, and we need to be sensitive to our own needs to determine when shifts are necessary.

The bottom line is: to be honest with yourself. Admit to yourself that it is okay not to be okay sometimes. It is perfectly fine to ask for help when you need it. You do not have to be strong all the time.

In this Chapter, we looked at self-care, why it is important, and the areas that need your attention so that you can thrive as a person and as a leader. With this, our discussion draws to an end, with our conclusion up next.

Conclusion

At the very beginning of the book, in the Preface, I shared how one of my first bosses first asked me to share my leadership skills with others. Since then, many people have encouraged me to do the same. Having mentored and coached rising leaders over the years, I realized there are simply not enough hours in the day for me to take the typical approach I prefer to take: personal, individualized, and customized to everyone's express needs so they realize their highest potential. With this realization and continued encouragement came the conviction that I had to write this book.

In Chapter One, we examined the dynamics involved in building high-performing teams. Recall that greatness comes from great leaders, teams, and organizations.

Then, in Chapter Two, we focused on matters to do

with selecting the ideal members of a great team - which are sometimes not the most obvious of selections. In my strategy, I shared how I'll pick a candidate of high character (such as integrity and genuineness), grit, and potential over one who has excellent certifications but is overly invested in optics and status. You learned how to create and establish your team (even before you make the first hire). We also looked at the steps that you can take to onboard, optimize pre-existing teams, and, when needed, offboard individuals.

After getting the right people on your team, you want your collection of great people to merge as one unit and become the team you envision. That was the focus of Chapter Three: Developing Your Team. We sequentially looked at the stages of team formation: Forming, Storming, Norming, Performing, and Adjourning (which I referred to as "Continuous Improvement"). Great teams I know all share several operating principles. We explored this collection of operating principles, which I dubbed "TTIPPC", and the acronym stands for "Transparency, Togetherness, Inclusion, Presence, Participation, Consistency". Just like in our own non-work related settings, interaction with others sometimes calls for different levels. The Group level, One-on-One, Accountability Pairs, Decompression Sessions, and Managing Up: were types or levels of interaction I utilized to develop my team.

Your team and my team do not function all by themselves. They are part of a larger ecosystem. Chapter 4 looked at how you could successfully collaborate or influence partners. We first looked at the different types of partners that you may need to interface with internally and externally. Then we explored how to define roles, and measures you can take to incorporate these partners as "Part of the Team", maintain these relations, and measure performance.

Planning something and getting something started is one thing. Developing it and sustaining it for months and years is a completely different matter. In Chapter Five, we focused on how to sustain your high-performing team. I shared with you the four elements I see as secrets to sustaining any relationships, including those that bind winning teams together. We gave each characteristic - Grace, safety, reciprocity, and resilience - a closer look.

Staying on course despite external and internal forces brought us to discuss the concept of maintaining alignment of the team's goals and objectives. It's not all about the organization or your team as a whole. Looking at the individual, what they want, and how you can help them realize their dreams is a magical ingredient in my strategy. We took a moment to explore that and spent time on providing development and performance feedback in a constructive and empathetic manner. We ended this chapter by discussing how you can motivate your team, manage transformational change, and deal with stress.

As we work at maintaining our teams, the need to monitor and assess performance becomes integral in understanding whether or not we are successful and we are how much and what we can do better to improve. For that reason, we looked at "Performance" in Chapter Six. Excellent, Good, and Poor performance require different approaches. We pinpointed those distinctions and how you could offer adequate recognition and rewards to your team members performing excellently or well. We also explored the difference in responses and consequences for each category of performer.

In the final chapter - Chapter Seven, we turned our attention back to you - the leader. It is easy to get caught up in the grind and myriad of responsibilities that you may have and neglect the one person who you will always need: yourself. In this chapter, we looked at aspects necessary for effective self-care. Establishing healthy boundaries, creating a good work-life balance, and taking good care of your mental, emotional, and physical health were the areas we dived into.

With each chapter, I closed with "My Message to You". I applaud you for getting this far! Oftentimes, I remind you that this work, like most great things, is hard. It requires great effort, patience, resilience, and sometimes - sacrifice. Is it worth it? That's for you to decide.

I can only speak for myself. In my 30+ years of leading teams in the business world, in the challenging and fast-evolving field of cybersecurity, there's always only been one answer. Yes.

Yes, it is worth it.

Every time.

Great leaders, great teams, and great organizations thrive with a human touch.

Grace and empathy are paramount to demonstrating your humanity. Scared to try it? Or think it's crazy? I dare you to add grace and empathy to your leadership toolbox and watch the magic happen. Remember the wise words of Peter Pan... "*all you need is faith, trust and a little Pixie dust*".

Glossary

CISO	Chief Information Security Officer
CISM	Certified Information Security Manager
CISSP	Certified Information Security Security Professional
CRISC	Certified in Risk and Information Systems Control
ISP	Internet Service Provider
OT	Operations Technology
PIP	Performance Improvement Plan
RACI Chart	Responsible, Accountable, Consulted and Informed

RFI		Request For Information
RFP		Request For Proposal
RFQ		Request For Quote
SMART		Specific, Measurable, Achievable, Relevant, Time-Bound

About the Author

Tammy Klotz is a Cybersecurity executive leader with over 30 years of leadership experience. She holds several certifications in Cybersecurity including CISM, CISSP, and CRISC certifications. She loves to serve and as such, the author is involved in several professional organizations, including the Lehigh Valley Chapter of Cloud Security Alliance, Delaware Valley Chapter of Women in Cybersecurity (WiCyS), Infragard, Evanta for CISOs by CISOs, the Cybersecurity Collaboration Forum, ISC2, and ISACA. Whilst serving at Covanta as Chief Information Security Officer, and Chief Technology Officer, she received the company's 2022 "Covanta Leadership Award". In 2023, she was named a Top 100 CISO by Cyber Defense Magazine. Tammy lives in Allentown, Pennsylvania, and has two successful daughters, Samantha and Erin.

The author is available for speaking engagements, and coaching or mentoring opportunities worldwide. She can be reached via Linkedin at

https://www.linkedin.com/in/tammyklotz/.

Made in United States
North Haven, CT
09 April 2024